WHO KNOWS?

Twelve Unsolved Mysteries

The yeti of the high Himalayas, the lost
civilisation of the Etruscans, the secret of the
hidden room at Glamis Castle, the strange
art of dowsing or water-divining – these are
among the unsolved historical and present-day
mysteries which have puzzled experts and
amateurs over the years, and to which no-one
yet knows the answers. Jacynth Hope-Simpson
describes twelve famous and much written
about mysteries and discusses the various
theories which have been offered as solutions.
Contemporary accounts, even those of eyewitnesses, often conflict, as anyone who has
ever had to try to describe an accident will
know, and further confusion is caused by
attempts to hide or distort facts. Mrs
Hope-Simpson presents all the evidence in a
lively and interesting way, and readers must
choose for themselves which theory seems
to be most plausible. This is a book to fascinate
and intrigue everyone who enjoys a mystery.

Who Knows?

Twelve Unsolved Mysteries
told by

Jacynth Hope-Simpson

Beaver Books

First published in 1974 by
William Heinemann Limited
15 Queen Street, Mayfair, London W1X 8BE
This paperback edition published in 1976 by
The Hamlyn Publishing Group Limited
London · New York · Sydney · Toronto
Astronaut House, Feltham, Middlesex, England

© Copyright Text Jacynth Hope-Simpson 1974
© Copyright Illustrations
The Hamlyn Publishing Group 1976
ISBN 0 600 39357 7

Printed in England by Cox & Wyman Limited
London, Reading and Fakenham
Set in Intertype Baskerville

Line drawings by John Glover
Cover illustration by Peter Connolly

Contents

Death by Witchcraft?

With any luck, the war would be over by midsummer. In the village of Lower Quinton, some of the effects of it had already passed. German bombers no longer came up the river valley on moonlit nights, using the thin silver line of the Avon to guide them to the big factories of Birmingham and Coventry. Most of the American soldiers who had been stationed nearby had left, to fight in the invasion of Europe. The girls missed them, if no-one else did. But there were still plenty of other signs of the war, including a large prisoner-of-war camp in the next village. Land girls in breeches worked on the farms while the young men were away fighting. There were shortages of everything, even a shortage of paper to wrap up your almost non-existent meat ration.

Petrol rationing made a difference. People like the doctor were able to get limited supplies, but many cars spent the war jacked up in garages with their tyres off. In any case, far fewer people than nowadays owned a car. They depended on the Midland Red bus, a bicycle or walking. This limited the distance that most of them ever travelled. You could walk happily through the lanes without fear of being run over, and the verges, without weed-killers or mechanical cutters, were high with flowers in the summer.

Warwickshire villages were smaller and more compact than they are now, without the spread of new housing that often threatens to swamp the original settlement. There was no television. The villages were basically as they had been for hundreds of years, separate and inward looking.

It was the year 1945, less than a generation ago, and in some ways a different world.

This was the world where an old man called Charles Walton was killed. His village of Lower Quinton was on the edge of the Avon valley, the country where Shakespeare spent his boyhood, just before the land rises to the Cotswolds.

In this country, the half-timbered and thatched cottages, such as that in which Walton lived, give place quite suddenly to the yellowy Cotswold limestone. Soon there are no more hedges, but dry stone walls, and within a mile or two the entire character of the country changes. Many people would rate it as one of the most picturesque parts of England.

It was on the slopes of Meon Hill, where the Cotswolds rise up from the Avon plain, that Walton's body was found on 14th February, 1945. A two-pronged hay-fork was pinned through either side of his neck, driven in with such force that the prongs went six inches into the ground. It later took two policemen to lift the fork out. The slash-hook which he had used for hedge cutting was still stuck in his body. His face had been cut, and on his throat and his chest were carved the sign of the cross.

There was no suggestion as to where to start looking.

Nothing was thought to be missing except that his watch-chain was there without the cheap tin 'turnip' watch that he normally wore. Yet surely the watch had not been a motive for murder?

The Warwickshire police, under Superintendent Spooner, tried to find out who were his particular friends and who were his possible enemies, but he seemed to have neither.

Walton was an old man of seventy-four, who had been a farm labourer all his active life. He still did occasional jobs when his rheumatism allowed, and he had been hedge cutting when he was killed. He was a widower and was looked after by his niece. Everyone agreed that he was not a sociable man, and he preferred to do his drinking at home, buying barrels of cider. Some village rumours said that he had quite a bit of money stored away.

Everyone agreed on one thing. This lonely man had a great affection for living creatures. He would talk to the birds, and claim they understood him. There was nothing at all in his pattern of life to suggest a motive for murder.

After two days, Scotland Yard was called in, and Detective Superintendent Robert Fabian took over the case. He was one of the best-known detectives of the day. Professor Webster of Birmingham, who was working on the post mortem, was another distinguished expert, so together they made a high-powered team. They had very little to work on. Walton's body had first been discovered, under a tree in a field, by his niece, a neighbour, and Farmer Potter for whom he was working. They had gone out to look for him when he did not come home. It was dark, and they had trampled all round the body. Potter had even tried to wrench the slash-hook out. When the police first arrived, they too had trampled in the February mud. It was going to be very hard to reconstruct what had happened.

The villagers denied any knowledge. They said that in such a small community someone would suspect if one of them was responsible. But, they implied, the police had not far to look. Only two miles away was a prison camp with over a thousand inmates.

Police inquiries there revealed that one of the men, an Italian, had been seen with blood on his clothes. Then news came that a baker's roundsman had seen a prisoner crouched in a ditch and scrubbing blood from his hands. His presence outside the camp was not in itself surprising. Italy was no longer at war with the Allies, so Italian prisoners were allowed out to work on the land. The man's coat was sent to Birmingham for laboratory tests, and the Royal Engineers went to search the ditch where the man had been seen. Their metal detectors found something. Then came anti-climax. What they had found was rabbit snares, and the blood on the coat was rabbit's blood. The man had simply been poaching.

By the time of the inquest, no progress at all had been made. It was not even possible to determine the last time that Walton had been seen. Potter thought he had seen him about midday, and perhaps again later. At least, he had caught a glimpse of a man in shirt sleeves, but he was vague and could not be pinned down to any exact time. In any case, Walton had been wearing a short-sleeved shirt. There was nothing to go on.

Then something trivial happened. Superintendent Fabian was walking on the slopes of Meon Hill in hopes of coming across some clue that he had not spotted before. It was nearly dusk when a black dog ran across his path. A few minutes later, a farm boy appeared.

'Looking for that dog?' Fabian asked.

'What dog, mister?'

'A black dog.'

The boy gasped, and ran away.

That evening, quite by chance, Fabian mentioned the episode in the village pub. One man was interested. He asked if Fabian was quite certain that it was a black dog. Then he told him a story, the usual preposterous-sounding legend of a young boy who saw a black dog eight nights in succession. For some reason, he was frightened. On the ninth night it turned into a headless woman, and next day his sister died.

The story was too absurd to take any notice of, except that Fabian, an extremely experienced investigator, sensed that as it was being told the entire mood in the pub changed. Soon afterwards, everyone left.

Normally that would have been the end of the matter. But, again entirely by chance, Fabian mentioned the black dog to an Inspector in the Warwickshire Police Traffic Department. He was reminded of something he had recently read in a book called *Folk Lore, Old Customs and Superstitions in Shakespeareland* by the Reverend Harvey Bloom.

In 1885 a young ploughboy had met a black dog eight nights in succession. On the ninth, it turned into a headless woman, and next day his sister died.

Here was the same story, except for one added detail: the ploughboy's name was Charles Walton. After a good deal of questioning, the police decided that it was the same man.

Their search took them not only to interviewing villagers, but into research on Warwickshire folklore and history. In Clive Holland's book *Warwickshire* (1906), they found an account of a murder in Long Compton, eleven miles from Lower Quinton. In 1875 a young man had murdered an old woman by stabbing her to death with a hayfork.

Here was the method of Charles Walton's murder in almost exact detail. The police, from having been stumbling along in a fog, must have felt themselves on the edge of some strange abyss. 'I pinned Ann Turner to the ground with a hayfork before slashing her throat with a billhook in the form of a cross,' the young man declared. His other words were still more disconcerting: 'Her was a proper witch.'

Of course, the police did not want to believe anything of the sort. All reason was against it. But as they searched, they found evidence that strong belief in witchcraft had lingered in the area until at least the time of Charles Walton's boyhood, the time when he was supposed to have seen the black dog. A few days after Walton's death, another black dog was discovered on Meon Hill. This time it had been hanged.

A strange silence came down on the villagers. They denied all knowledge of Walton's death, and it seemed as if they had entered into a conspiracy not to speak. This lasted for the rest of the investigation.

So the police pressed on, following lines of inquiry far removed from those of the usual murder. They read stories of phantom coaches and headless horses. None of these had much to do with the investigation, unless it were that by long brooding about these things someone had turned his reason. Then there were stories of crops failing and animals dying, and witches being blamed. Many of these had been current in the lifetime of the older men and women of Lower Quinton.

The police learnt too about the Rollright Stones, a prehistoric stone circle as large as the outer circle of Stonehenge and probably older. For centuries past, it had been a traditional place for witches to perform their rites, and it seems still to be used. In a book on witchcraft published in 1965, twenty years after the murder, Justine Glass writes, 'I have seen traces of ritual witch fires, roughly in the centre of the circle.' The Rollright Stones are on the edge of the Cotswolds, near the village of Long Compton where that other hayfork murder had taken place.

What, if anything, did this background of superstition add up to? Here someone joined in the investigation who was very different from the normal detective. It was Dr Margaret Murray, a former Professor of Egyptology at the University of London. Dr Murray, who lived to be over a hundred, was, among her other attainments, one of the leading authorities in the world upon witchcraft.

Many people assume that witchcraft is simply a blasphemy on Christianity, as expressed by saying the Lord's Prayer backwards. Dr Murray and other scholars have shown that it seems to be basically a very much older religion, not merely pre-Christian but pre-Greek and pre-Roman as well, going right back, perhaps, to the days of the prehistoric painted caves. In its earliest origins, it was a fertility cult, and its object was to ensure the continuing fertility of human beings and of the crops. When other religions, such as Christianity came in, they did not, it is now thought, supersede the 'Old Religion'. There seems to be much evidence for its continuing through the Middle Ages. One suggestion often cited is that some of the strange carvings which can be found in odd corners of mediaeval churches may be the symbols of the witch cult.

13

In the sixteenth, and still more in the seventeenth centuries, the witches were rigorously persecuted by those who took literally the command in the Bible, 'Thou shalt not suffer a witch to live.' After that, the cult was assumed to have been stamped out, but now, as the police were finding, the belief was still alive in the twentieth century. On the one hand were old country people in their remote villages. On the other hand were educated people who had taken to studying witchcraft and who claimed at times to practise it. The new kind of witches, if one may call them that, were often the sort of people who might also be interested in mystical Eastern religions or the effects of drugs.

Margaret Murray spent a week at Lower Quinton, pretending to be an artist sketching, which helped her to talk to people. She came away 'ninety-five per cent certain' that Walton's death had been caused by witchcraft. Five years after the murder she put her ideas on record in *The Birmingham Post*.

'I think there are still remnants of witchcraft in isolated parts of Great Britain. I believe Charles Walton was one of the people sacrificed. . . .

'The belief is that if life is taken out of the ground through farming it must be replaced by a blood sacrifice.

'I am not interested in the murder, only in the witches. I think it was a murder without normal motive – no money was missing and there was no other reason why the old man should have been killed.

'He died in February, one of the four months in the year when sacrifices are carried out. February's sacrificial day was the second. Old Walton was murdered on 14th February, but the old calendar was twelve days behind ours, which brings the date back to 2nd February.'

So five years after the murder, it had still not been solved, in spite of intensive if traditional police work. This included literally hundreds of interviews and the taking of aerial photographs to make a large scale map on which the movements of many people could be charted in detail.

Time went on, and still the murderer could not be found. For the next fifteen years, until his retirement, Superintendent Spooner of the Warwickshire Police went each year to the scene of Walton's death on the anniversary of the crime. His hope was that his patience would wear the murderer down. 'There may be a simple explanation for the crime,' he said, 'but the motive could equally be a fantastic one. The villagers are frightened to talk. That was our trouble right through the investigations.'

During those years, some strange clues turned up. In 1949 a witches' sabbath was said to have been held at the Rollright Stones. This added to the belief that the witchcraft lingered on in the district. Then in the 1950's a woman whose name has never been published made a statement to the Sunday newspaper *Reynolds' News*. She claimed to know that Walton's death had been a sacrificial killing in order to preserve the fertility of the soil. She said that the actual murderer was a woman brought by car from another part of the country. When the police questioned her, she would not say anything definite, claiming that she was 'crazy with fear'. Later, however, she gave an interview to the *Daily Mirror* in which she said Walton's body had been held down with a pitchfork in order that his blood could run into the soil.

Obviously, this could be the sort of near-lunatic confession that murders tend to attract. If several people really came by car, it is strange that all the detailed police inquiries should not have unearthed any mention of the fact. A car at that time would have been much more noticeable than it would now. Nothing came of her statement.

But there were a few happenings locally which perhaps were straws in the wind. In 1960 a watch was discovered in what had been Walton's back garden. It was thought to be the one missing from his body, but a local man remarked it was strange it no longer contained his bit of polished black glass. Nobody knows what the black glass was for, but it has been suggested it might have been a witch's mirror for seeing the future in.

Other facts came up about Walton, such as his sympathy for birds and animals to a degree that many people found uncanny. To this must be added memories of his having seen the black dog as a boy, which again helped set him apart from his fellows. It was said that at one time he had played with toads. He would 'tie a toy plough to its legs and let it run towing the thing across a field'. One man at least in the district used to get 'real scared and mad'.

It sounds a harmless enough prank, except from the point of view of the toad. But did anybody who heard of it have a folk memory of a seventeenth-century belief? The Scottish witch, Isobel Gowdie, had declared that if a toy plough harnessed with toads was pulled across the fields the land would become barren.

In other words, should the whole theory be turned upside down? Could it be that Walton was killed not by people practising witchcraft, but by someone, almost certainly a local man, who suspected him of practising witchcraft himself? Did someone think he could have harmed their crops, their animals, or even perhaps themselves? Did the villagers suddenly realise what had happened, and did this explain their silence?

It is not necessary to believe in witchcraft to think that it played some part in Walton's killing. The only question is whether or not the killer believed, and did this supply a motive? If so, which way round was it? Was Walton simply a victim, or was he suspected of witchcraft himself? Is there any significance in the date?

It was the day of the old Druid ceremonies, and of the Roman feast of the Lupercalia on which dogs were sacrificed. In the Christian calendar, it was Saint Valentine's Day, when the birds to which Walton was so attached are said to choose their mates for the year. In 1945 it was also Ash Wednesday, the day of penitence and purification at the beginning of Lent.

And finally, for what insane reason did the killer carve the sign of the cross?

In Search of the Lost World

'You need have no fear of any failure.'

These words were written, in a letter to his wife, by a man setting out on an expedition in 1925. No more has ever been heard of him, but the argument as to what happened to him still goes on.

The man was called Percy Fawcett. By profession, he was a Lieutenant Colonel in the Royal Artillery; by choice he was a trained surveyor, an exhibitor at the Royal Academy, a county cricketer and a designer of racing yachts; by nature he was a mystic and a born explorer.

Before the first World War, he had escaped from the monotony of Army life when he was sent as official surveyor to chart the disputed boundaries between Brazil, Bolivia and Peru. At times, he was working at over fifteen thousand feet, scrambling along paths beside a razor-backed ridge that fell to a sheer drop thousands of feet below. He descended to the Amazon forests, where rain fell so heavily that it came down as solid water.

Fawcett, who was a man of great stamina, and unusually resistant to fever, found this exhilarating.

After the war, he was anxious to return to South

America. He thought that Britain was 'on the wane' and he saw South America as the sub-continent of the future. It was also, and to an extent that was to obsess him, the sub-continent of the past.

In the course of his travels, Fawcett had seen and heard many strange things. South America has been subject to giant volcanic upheavals in the past, which is why the fossils of sea creatures can be found high in the Andes. Fawcett thought, wrongly in the view of modern scholars, that the ancient city of Tiahuanco, near Lake Titicaca in the Andes, had been raised up to its present height in one of these upheavals. He found Tiahuanco a mystery, with its huge blocks of stone so tightly fitting 'that it is impossible to insert a knife blade between the mortarless joins'.

But he was convinced there were far more mysterious places. His conviction was based on a document in the National Library of Brazil at Rio de Janeiro. It tells of how a party of six Portuguese and a dozen Indians set out to look for lost gold and silver mines in 1743. They came to a point where mountains, as sheer as a cliff and gleaming with quartz, rose out of a grassy plain. It was some time before they found a crevice which led to a way up. At the top was a high plain, and four or five miles in the distance a great city. There was no sign of life.

When they dared to approach it cautiously, they found that the place was deserted. It was built of huge blocks of stone, with the buildings carved with figures and the statue of a man on a column in the central square. On the outskirts was a vast hall, with fifteen rooms off it, and in each was a carved serpent's head with water flowing out of its mouth.

The explorers left. A few days later, they caught sight of two white men in a canoe, but failed to attract their attention. They sent an account of what they had seen to the coast by an Indian runner, but nobody knows what became of the party, or if they ever returned to the city.

One attempt to find the city during the nineteenth century came to nothing. Then in 1911, Hiram Bingham found the lost Inca city of Machu Picchu, forgotten for hundreds of years. The idea of other cities became more plausible. Fawcett's interest was further whetted by an odd circumstance.

The novelist Rider Haggard wrote one of the best of all thrillers based on the secrets of the past in *King Solomon's Mines*. It was he who gave Colonel Fawcett a black basalt figure about ten inches high, which he had obtained from Brazil. After many experts had failed to identify it, Fawcett consulted a psychometrist, a person sensitive to the vibrations the figure gave off.

He had a vision of an ancient city in South America, of volcanic eruptions and earthquakes, of people taking refuge up in the hills. This confirmed Fawcett in his belief in lost cities. The city was surrounded, he thought, by impenetrable swamp, by grass so tall that no-one could pass through it, and the area inhabited by species that had survived nowhere else in the world. As well as this there might be a belt of land without any water, to make the city still more inaccessible. To this city, he gave the name of 'Z'.

Fawcett's belief in the city was strengthened by stories he had heard of houses with 'stars to light them which never went out'. The stories were widespread, and the Indians were afraid to approach these buildings with their constantly shining lights that seemed to give out no warmth. Fawcett believed that the people who built the city had discovered a means of lighting that was unknown to modern science.

Another lost secret of the early American people was, he thought, a liquid used for softening blocks of stone. He gave this as an explanation of how the Incas had joined huge stones together with such precision.

Not only did he believe in the city, he thought he knew where it was. Only three men did so. 'One was a Frenchman, whose last attempt to get there cost him an eye, and it is probable he will make no more; the second is an Englishman who before he left the country was suffering from an advanced stage of cancer, and is probably no longer alive; the third is the writer.'

A secret known to three people only. An unapproachable city set high on a plateau. Mysterious white people. Lost secrets of science. The hope of 'giving to the world the story of the most stupendous discovery of modern times'. It all has the ring of a boys' adventure story of the period. In particular, the high plateau up on its mountain ramparts, the hints about creatures elsewhere extinct: this is exactly the setting of Conan Doyle's book *The Lost World*.

In his *Life of Sir Arthur Conan Doyle*, John Dickson Carr says that the idea came from the footsteps of an iguanodon found near Conan Doyle's Sussex home, and from a book on prehistoric animals. But Fawcett also claims credit for the story. He said he showed Conan Doyle photographs of 'the Ricardo Franco hills, flat-topped and mysterious. They stood like a lost world, forested to their tops, and the imagination could picture the last vestiges there of an age long vanished.' Conan Doyle asked him for more information, and 'the fruit of it was his *Lost World* in 1912'.

It was not until after the first World War, in which he served with distinction and won a D.S.O., that Fawcett managed to set off to look for his city. In the past, he had often been unlucky in his choice of companions, so on this occasion he took with him simply his elder son, Jack, a young man who made a cult of physical fitness, and Jack's friend, Raleigh Rimell.

As later commentators have pointed out, both young men were totally inexperienced in such ventures. They set off from Sao Paulo in Brazil early in 1925. Fawcett was sustained by more stories of Indians who had seen cities in the jungle. He tried to fight down his doubts about Rimell, who proved to be badly affected by insect bites, and who obstinately refused to learn a single word of Portuguese. In May 1925, Fawcett sent a letter from a place called Dead Horse Camp, and wrote, 'You need have no fear of any failure.' After that, there was silence.

Nobody was surprised. He was setting off on a journey which could easily take two years. His route would take him across three of the southern tributaries of the Amazon, which join the river near to its mouth. In his book on the Amazon, Robin Furneaux calls this journey 'one of the most difficult and dangerous ever undertaken in the history of exploration'.

At that time, the usual way of penetrating the country was to travel by river. Nowadays, there are also landing strips for aircraft. To go by land, seeking food as one went, for Fawcett carried very few supplies, was by far the most difficult way. Once away from the rivers, it might be hard to find water. There were few viewpoints or landmarks to help in picking out the direction. The rivers were often hidden amongst jungle, through which it was necessary to push and slash in order to make any progress.

The writer Peter Fleming, who is not given to over-estimating difficulties, was later to write, 'We struggled in those dense and jagged thickets with a horrible feeling of impotence, as wasps must struggle in marmalade.'

Time went past, and anxiety for Fawcett increased. Inquiries among the few officials of the Brazilian government who lived in the area yielded nothing. A French civil engineer, however, told Fawcett's younger son that he had met an old man in Brazil who said that his name was Fawcett. At that time, he had never heard of the Colonel's disappearance, and so he made little of it.

It was partly on the strength of this report that in 1928, three years after Fawcett's departure, the American press sponsored the first expedition to look for him. It was led by Commander George Dyott, who took with him two photographers, two radio experts, and a back-up team of twenty-six men, sixty-four bullocks, ten mules and appropriate amounts of equipment. An Indian guided them from Dead Horse Camp, through scrubland where even the mules suffered from the knife-edged grass. Then they went down river to a village of the Anauqua Indians. The chieftain's child wore a trinket around his neck, a metal plate inscribed with the name of a London firm which had supplied Fawcett's luggage.

The chief then took Dyott another three days' journey, through country inhabited by the Suya Indians who had the reputation of being savage. Indeed, the chief indicated that they might have murdered Fawcett, and performed a grisly reconstruction, which ended with his yelling, 'Suya! Bang, bang, bang!'

Then they reached the territory of the Kalapolo Indians, who said that Fawcett had stayed with them for a night. They made signs to show that for several days afterwards they had seen smoke from his fires, but this had then stopped.

This feature had puzzled later commentators, as there is no high ground in the area from which distant smoke could be seen. The Kalapolos told Dyott that the Anauquas might have killed Fawcett. Dyott then decided to rejoin the main body of his party, before setting out on the next stage of his journey. This he was never able to accomplish. The mood of the local Indians grew menacing, and Dyott was forced to escape down the Xingu river by night in a light canoe.

The next event in the Fawcett saga was when a Swiss trapper called Stefan Rattin turned up at the British Consulate in Sao Paulo. He said he had met a white man, with blue eyes and a long beard, in an Indian village. The man, who was dressed in skins, took advantage of a drinking bout among the Indians to tell Rattin that he was an English colonel, and that he was being kept prisoner. He had a few personal possessions, such as a signet ring and a locket with a photograph of a woman and two children.

When Rattin asked if he was alone, he said that his son was sleeping, and started to cry. He asked Rattin to tell the British authorities of his plight, and Rattin accordingly set out on a five month journey to Sao Paulo. He swore that at the time of meeting the man he had never so much as heard of Colonel Fawcett.

The story attracted an enormous amount of attention. The place was all wrong: some three hundred miles from where Fawcett had last been heard of. The eye colour was wrong, and why should the man have long hair when Fawcett himself had been bald from an early age? On the other hand, the details of the signet ring were convincing.

No explanation was offered as to why Fawcett, who spoke Spanish and Portuguese fluently, should not have spoken these languages since Rattin's English was very poor, unless, of course, it was to make the chance of being

understood by the Indians much less likely. Why, when Rattin was using a pencil, had he not taken the chance of sending a written message? On the other hand, the man had mentioned someone called Paget, and this was the name of a friend who had helped to finance Fawcett's expedition. If it was all a hoax, what did Rattin hope to get out of it? Shortly afterwards, he disappeared, saying that he was going to rescue the Colonel. He was never heard of again.

By this time, so far as Brazil was concerned, Colonel Fawcett had become a part of local folklore. So many stories had grown up about him that anyone hearing his name for the first time might have been forgiven for wondering if he had really existed at all. At this stage, an English expedition was mounted to try to find out what had happened to Fawcett. One of the members, who went along as special correspondent for *The Times*, was a young man called Peter Fleming.

The expedition produced the theme of an extremely witty travel book, *Brazilian Adventure*. Peter Fleming set out to ridicule the clichés, then popular among travel writers, about 'the Depths of the Savage Jungle', and to show that 'exploring the Mato Grosso is a soft option compared with caravanning in the Cotswolds'.

He managed to do this, and yet at the same time convey the remoteness and the discomfort, the exhaustion and the worry, of life on the banks of the Amazon and its tributaries. At that point, in the early 1930's, the existing maps of the region could best be classified as works of the imagination. Unfortunately, the expedition made no real attempt to find Fawcett, and much of the comedy is provided by the slow realisation that their leader never really intended to do so.

In one of the more serious moments in the book, Fleming offers his own suggestion as to what had become of Fawcett. Having himself attempted a cross-country journey, he knew the difficulty of finding food and water and of striking the rivers which were the main highways. He thought Fawcett and his companions, one of whom, at least, was lame, were either killed or had died of hunger, thirst and exhaustion. If they had been imprisoned, they would surely have died of the extreme hardship of Indian life. He said that Fawcett, although the oldest, was physically the toughest and was the likeliest to have survived. Even so, he put the odds at a 'million to one chance', and thought that if Fawcett were still alive he had probably become mentally deranged.

More rumours of white men living among Indians followed, along with various telepathic communications purporting to come from Fawcett. In 1933, a compass belonging to Fawcett was found in the territory of the

Bakairi Indians, some one hundred and fifty miles from where he was thought to have been. There were various rumours about a white boy, living with the Indians, who was said to be Jack Fawcett's son. Then, in 1950, some new evidence was advanced.

Orlando Villas Boas is a man who has dedicated his life to Brazilian Indians, whose own traditional way of life, indeed whose very existence, is now being threatened. Having lived for a year with the Kalapolo tribe, he became convinced that they had killed Fawcett. In the end, they admitted to it. The reason given was that Fawcett had insulted an Indian and slapped his face. The Kalapolo chief showed Villas Boas a grave.

He said that the three Englishmen had been killed together and then thrown into a lagoon. A few days later, Fawcett's body was taken out and buried. The bones were duly exhumed and sent home to London, where they were examined at the Royal Anthropological Institute. They were found to be of a man about five feet seven in height, shorter than anyone in the expedition, and were probably those of an Indian.

A party which included Fawcett's younger son, Brian, set out to inspect the grave. They never arrived at the truth of the matter. Brian Fawcett remained convinced that his father had in fact gone to the country of the Bakairi Indians where his compass was found. This was partly because one of Fawcett's last letters had mentioned a Bakairi who told him about a big waterfall, with a strange inscription half hidden on the rocks. Fawcett had been determined to visit it.

On the other hand, if he did go to the Bakairi country, this would suggest that the map references he had given before his disappearance were all incorrect, and that the men trying to find him were working on false data. It is unlikely that an experienced surveyor, who was a Founder's Medallist of the Royal Geographical Society, would make such a mistake, unless, of course, Fawcett had done it on purpose in order to try to conceal the whereabouts of his lost city.

It is very hard to know what to make of the Kalapolo tribe's confession, in view of the fact that the bones they claimed to be Fawcett's are clearly not his at all. It remains that of the three tribes which may have been involved in his death – the Anauqua, the Kalapolo and the Suya Indians – the Kalapolos are the only ones who have ever admitted anything.

As happens with many mysteries, as the eyewitnesses die the chance of our ever knowing the truth becomes less year by year. Fawcett himself would be dead by now in any circumstances. His son, Jack, was born just after the turn of the century. If he had lived in England, he could very well still be alive, but the chance of his having survived in Brazil and still being found is now too remote to be worth considering.

In 1953, Brian Fawcett published his father's writings, which make, as one might expect, an excellent adventure story. At that time, Brian Fawcett still clung to the belief that his father might have found an ancient city and be living there. 'If the tradition is true that the last remnants of the ancient race had indeed protected their sanctuary by ringing themselves round with fierce savages, what chance would there be of returning?'

This statement might be expected from his father's son, for Fawcett's own writings show a combination of great practical skill and courage with a willingness, indeed eagerness, to believe strange things that is somehow very appealing. A recent British Ambassador to Brazil described Fawcett as being 'as credulous an old dear as ever bought a gold brick'.

Or was he entirely? Belief in a great city, often called El Dorado, the golden one, goes right back to the very first days of Europeans in South America. It was thought that it might have been founded by people who had fled from the conquering Incas a hundred years earlier.

The first search for El Dorado was in 1531, and there were repeated expeditions for the rest of the sixteenth century. Sir Walter Raleigh went twice in search of the city, and staked his reputation on finding it. The French and the Dutch joined the search, and it went on during the eighteenth and nineteenth centuries. There had been an expedition to look for it in 1908, and as well as Fawcett's there was another in 1925. At the very least, one must say that Fawcett was not alone.

How about other reports of cities? One hears of 'great snow peaks looming above the clouds more than two miles overhead; gigantic precipices of many-coloured granite rising sheer thousands of feet above the foaming, glistening, roaring rapids'. In such a setting there is said to be a deserted city, rising in terrace after terrace, with over a hundred stairways and 'a maze of beautiful granite houses'.

Other reports make even more startling claims. 'For several more days we explored this ancient sanctuary that stretched for many miles across the mountains. . . . The numerous groups, each a little city in itself, revealed this to be a great metropolis, perhaps the largest in South America. . . . Checking our findings carefully with engineers in Chachapoyas, the size of the colossus was determined to be some sixty square miles – 70,000 acres of continuous ruins.'

Who Knows?

Or again, 'At 9200 feet we came to a spot known as Monja Tranca. What I saw amazed me – a big circular building with carefully structured fretwork. And there were many more such buildings. Wanting to see how far they extended, we tramped along through the sharp thorns and thick vegetation for many hours. There seemed to be no end of them. In all, we explored thirteen different sites, all containing important ruins.'

If descriptions like this were found in an obscure manuscript, written by some early traveller, many people would dismiss them as fantasy. Yet the first description, the city set among mountains, is in the words of Hiram Bingham who found the lost Inca city of Machu Picchu. Nowadays, Machu Picchu is famous, even to the extent of having a tourist hotel, and it vies with Delphi as one of the most romantically beautiful, not to say most photographed, ruins in all the world.

The other accounts are of the work of Gene Savoy and other members of the Andean Explorers Club. In the 1960's they mounted a series of 'El Dorado' expeditions to look for lost cities. They went into the jungle very high in the Andes, where the tree line is much higher than in the Alps, and explored the upper parts of the Amazon Basin. No-one believed that this region had ever been inhabited by any advanced civilisation, apart, perhaps, from the natives of the area who warned them of enchantments and who refused to venture far from their own settlements. The explorers found the remains of road systems through the jungles, and not merely one city but about forty cities with 'very sophisticated architecture' and 'advanced technical skills'.

All this was found within a comparatively small area; the entire Amazon forest extends for about three million square miles and parts of it are the least explored region of the world today. No-one can tell how much more there is to discover. It seems obvious nowadays that Fawcett was wrong in looking for his lost city towards the mouth of the Amazon for it has been fairly conclusively shown that there is nothing of the sort around there. But had he returned to the Andes, where once he did his surveying work, he might have found his lost city after all.

Is it Abominable?

He is the spirit of men killed violently. If you see him, you may die yourself. Shooting at him will not help, for a bullet will only pass through him. Or can you escape? There are said to be cases where he has been scared away by the loud blowing of conch shells and long horns. Tibetan children are told to run downhill if he chases them, because the long hair falling into his eyes may confuse him. Another theory is that you can render him harmless by making him get drunk.

These are just a few of the legends about the yeti, otherwise known as the Abominable Snowman.

It is easy enough to see how legends grow up in the Himalayas. Men are living and working there at altitudes as high as the highest peaks in Europe. Other mountain peaks soar high above them. They live in small, isolated communities, with little to protect them from the harsh weather.

It is no wonder that for them the vast expanses of untouched snow are the home of spirits, nor that when the earth shakes and the air vibrates with avalanches they should fear the power of devils. In this world spiritual things take on great importance. Prayer flags flutter outside the villages. Services are chanted in dark smoke-laden, Buddhist monasteries until the senses reel.

It is inevitable that strange stories should have arisen here, and that the inhabitants should have come to imagine some wild creature of the snows. To support these beliefs successive groups of explorers also think the Abominable Snowman may exist.

The yeti's first public appearance in Europe was in a book by Lieutenant Colonel L. A. Waddell called *Among the Himalayas*, published in 1898, in which he claimed to have seen one near Sikkim nine years previously. After that, no more was heard until 1921 when a reconnaissance expedition went to study the prospects of climbing Mount Everest. This was the first of eleven expeditions, nine British and two Swiss, until the mountain was finally conquered thirty years later.

The Sherpas who accompanied this 1921 expedition claimed to have seen a yeti, and the following year a lama at the Rongbuk monastery told climbers that there were five of 'these wild men' in the area. In the book *Mount Everest: The Reconnaissance 1921*, Lieutenant Colonel C. K. Howard-Bury spoke of seeing tracks like those of a 'laughing wolf' at twenty thousand feet. This was the start of real interest in the creature.

The 1920's was a heroic age of Everest climbing. In those days there were fewer of the technical aids that climbers enjoyed later. It was the period when Mallory and Irvine disappeared, heading towards the summit, and nobody knows even now if they ever reached it before they died. One of the few survivors of these expeditions is Howard Somervell, who was counted as one of the strongest climbers of his generation and went up to a record of over

twenty-eight thousand feet without oxygen. He was also a distinguished medical missionary and a talented painter. He serves as a living reminder that Everest climbers are not simply a random group of tourists but members of a very small élite. In other words they are men whose opinions and observations are not to be lightly dismissed.

Somervell says that there is no doubt at all that belief in the yeti is general among the native inhabitants of the Himalayas, but like most Europeans he dismisses any idea of his being a wild man of the snows. 'My own view is that it is probably a species of Langur, a kind of large monkey. Obviously very shy, as so few people have seen it, though many more *say* they have. At a monastery near the Tibetan border I was shown a yeti's scalp. I thought it was probably pigskin. I've been pointed out yeti tracks several times by Sherpas but normally I thought them due to the Himalayan fox, which when galloping makes tracks with

all four feet near together which are about the right distance apart for a man's stride.'

Another famous between-the-wars climber was Frank S. Smythe. In 1937, he saw a strange track and measured it while his porters 'huddled together, a prey to that curious sullenness which in the Tibetan means fear'. The creature had a stride of from eighteen inches to two feet, less going uphill, and the traces showed the clear imprint of five toes. It crossed gullies and glaciers like an expert climber. For a moment, Smythe was caught on his own in the mist, with no sight or sound of anybody around him. He uneasily remembered the story that to catch sight of the yeti could bring about one's own death.

Smythe's notes and photographs were examined at the Zoological Society and the Natural History Museum, where experts determined that the tracks were probably those of some species of bear. Smythe wrote an article in *The Times* 'debunking' the yeti legend, and the many hostile letters that he received showed how the British public had taken the Abominable Snowman to its heart. In his book *The Valley of Flowers*, he was apologetic about this. He said that while he now believed the tracks he had seen were those of a bear, he hoped there might yet prove to be an Abominable Snow Man, an Abominable Snow Woman, 'and not least of all, an Abominable Snow Baby'.

The second World War meant a complete break in Everest expeditions. Then, in 1951, there was another reconnaissance to assess the chances of climbing the mountain from the Nepalese side, instead of from Tibet as before the war.

It might have been thought that the last had been heard of the yeti, but in December 1951 his name reappeared in *The Times*. Eric Shipton, the leader of the expedition, saw what the native Sherpa Sen Tensing (not the same man as finally climbed Everest) called the tracks of a yeti. The tracks had three broad toes and what looked like a broad thumb. The creature evidently jumped over crevasses using his toes to grip on the other side.

Tensing said that he had seen a yeti two years before from about twenty-five yards away. He said he was half man and half beast, and, except for the face which was hairless, was covered with reddish brown hair. His view was that the creature seemed frightened of men. On 7th December, 1951, *The Times* printed a photograph of the footprint which has often been reproduced since. It clearly showed the toe marks, and an ice axe set beside it helps to establish the size which is about twelve and a half inches.

Other climbers at this time saw traces of the yeti. In 1951, Edmund Hillary was climbing at nineteen thousand feet when his Sherpas found a tuft of long, black hairs. 'They looked more like bristles than anything else,' Hillary commented. He and a fellow climber George Lowe were eagerly discussing taking the hairs back home when one of the Sherpas divined their intention, snatched the tuft of hairs, and flung it away.

'Our scientific interest wasn't sufficiently great to make us climb down a couple of hundred feet to find it,' wrote Hillary. Later, he may have regretted this when he set off on a world tour with an alleged yeti scalp.

In 1953, Hillary was able to tell his companions, 'Well, we knocked the bastard off,' which was one way of saying that Everest had been climbed. The yeti retained its appeal to the British public, and the most responsible people were taking it seriously. Showell Styles, who has seen footprints which Sherpas told him were made by a yeti, summed up these views when he said, 'I'm quite sure the Sherpas were telling the truth, and equally sure that there *is* some strange beast that walks on two legs in the high snows and has never been caught or identified.' Then came a claim from a European that he had actually seen it.

On an expedition to Annapurna, Don Whillans saw a dark object which caused two lines of crows to fly up. In almost alarmingly matter-of-fact tones, his Sherpas said that it was a yeti. Night was falling and he did not pursue it. Next morning, he found a set of deep tracks of about the same size foot as his own, a man's size six. The tracks came down to about thirteen thousand feet, and vanished over a crest at about fifteen thousand. He rejected the idea that they might have been made by a bear.

Next night, he looked out by moonlight and saw a dark, moving shape. He could distinguish limbs, and 'a kind of bounding movement'. It was going uphill on all fours, and gave the impression that it was hunting for food. It seemed to be an ape-like creature. When it disappeared Whillans said that the odd, uneasy atmosphere of the place disappeared with it.

His disquiet, like that felt by Smythe, poses a question. Obviously, these mountaineers are men of great physical courage, but are they affected by the atmosphere of the high Himalayas, so that they see things differently from the way that they would at lower heights? The loneliness, the sheer scale of the place, the dangers among which they live, may have more effect upon them than they are prepared to admit.

Then there is the question of rarefied air. Dr Michael Ward, a member of the successful Everest expedition, has made further trips to the Himalayas to study the physical effects of high altitude. It has been known since the sixteenth century that great height affects people's breathing and power to move. As well as the physical effects, Ward describes nightmares and inability to distinguish the exact whereabouts of certain objects.

He says, 'There is nothing that I have ever encountered that is anything like the fatigue of high altitude. It is relentless, inescapable, and all embracing. No other mental or physical stress has anything in common with it. The feeling of impending dissolution is indescribable.' In these circumstances, could the judgement of the climbers have been affected by the Sherpas' own fears?

Against this easy explanation is the sheer weight of the testimony. The latest comes in 1973 in the zoological journal, *Oryx*, from J. A. McNeely, E. W. Cronin, and H. B. Emery who declare their confirmed belief in the yeti. They point out that there are over fifty descriptions or photographs of footprints which tend to be consistent. So do descriptions of the animal provided by mountain people.

The yeti seems to be rather less than the height of a man, with short coarse hair that is reddish or greyish brown. Its face is hairless, and it has long arms and big feet.

The article in *Oryx* offers an explanation of one puzzling fact. What can the yeti find up in the snows to live on? The authors suggest that the creature spends most of its time in dense forests below the snow line and that the tracks are only found when it goes up over the mountain passes from one forest to another.

As for its nature, they favour the theory that it is a descendant of the giant ape *Gigantopithecus*, known only in fossil form. Certainly, strange survivals are possible, the standard example being the fish called the coelacanth. This was thought to have become extinct some fifty million years ago, but since 1938 a number of living specimens have been caught. It has been described as 'a living fossil'. The yeti might be such another.

Shy and elusive though it is, it may be only a matter of time until someone captures a creature which corresponds with the yeti. Don Whillans has an interesting comment on this.

'I am convinced that they [the Sherpas] believe the yeti does exist, that it is some kind of sacred animal that is best left alone; that if you don't bother it, it won't bother you. I feel very much the same way myself. If it's not a bear and is one of these legendary creatures, and if it's managed to survive so long and under such bitterly cold conditions, it deserves to be left alone.'

The Guardian of the Treasure

'Dreadful is that place.'

These are strange words to find written over the door of a church. To enter is stranger still. There is the holy water stoup, but the creature supporting it is none other than a lame demon. Crowded all round the walls of the church are vividly coloured pictures, done in minute detail, which give an impression not of peace but of restlessness and unease. What exactly is this place, and how did it come to be here?

It is not, as one might imagine, a church in some rich city where there is money to spare for such extravagant work. Instead, it is a poor and remote hill village on the French side of the Pyrenees, called Rennes-le-Château. It is savage country. The earth plunges down into crevasses or rises to mountains with outcrops of rock in which one may make out the shape of human faces. The air is scented with thyme and with rosemary, the only figures in sight may be a goatherd or shepherd leading his flock. In distance, the tourist resorts of the French and Spanish coast are only some fifty miles away; in time, they might be two thousand years.

So why, the question comes again, why this strange, perturbing church in such a remote village? The style of the decorations is that of the last century, but at that time the village was said to have had only two hundred inhabitants. Nowadays, it has even fewer. So why should somebody spend so much money, and why in such a puzzling way?

Some people have thought that the answer may lie very deep in the past, and that the church itself can provide the answer.

Rennes-le-Château, or Aereda as it once was, has not always been a tiny village right off the map. In early times, this was a prosperous area. The wild mountain country around is rich in minerals like lead, gold, copper, nickel and sulphur. Silver abounds in such wealth that the Phoenicians are supposed to have used it to make anchors.

The country is also full of mineral springs, both hot and cold. Even before Roman times, there was a settlement at Rennes. The Romans, who called the place Reddae, drove a road through the town to their Spanish province, and built elaborate public baths nearby. Originally, these were only a suburb of Reddae, but now they are Rennes-les-Bains, Rennes Spa, and a much bigger place than Rennes-le-Château.

The Roman empire fell to the barbarians in the fifth century, and the Vandals and the Visigoths plundered Rome. They were wandering tribes, and soon came to both sides of the Pyrenees, where their principal cities included Toledo in what is now Spain, and Reddae, or Rennes-le-Château. It was important because of its position on the route over the Pyrenees, and its high situation made it easy to defend. At that time, the population may have been as many as thirty thousand.

The Visigoths fell in turn to the Franks. In the Middle Ages, the overlords of the territory were the Knights Templar, the order dedicated to guarding the Temple of Jerusalem. They brought in German miners to work the gold mines, but some whispered that the men were not digging the gold so much as melting it down. Two hundred years later, there were similar stories, of false money being coined in the district using no-one knew what source of precious metal.

This was a time of warring small kingdoms, and great feudal families, and in the fourteenth century the lower half of the town of Rennes-le-Château was destroyed in a siege. Only the highest part remained, and after the town had been pillaged, an outbreak of plague carried off many of the survivors. From that day to this, Rennes has been no more than a village.

Still there were occasional rumours of gold finds. In the 1640's a young shepherd in search of a lost sheep claimed to have found a cave guarded by skeletons and filled with piles of gold. No-one believed his story. He was accused of stealing the gold and was stoned to death.

During these years, the country around Rennes became the property of a succession of noble families; Hautpoul, Blanchefort, Fleury. It became more and more remote until it seems to have been forgotten. In 1885, when the Bishop of Carcassonne wanted to punish a priest for his too forthright opinions, he sent him to Rennes-le-Château as if into exile.

This priest was a man of thirty-three called Bérenger Saumière. He was the son of a peasant family, without money or influence, and his banishment must have seemed the end of all hope for him. The village was dwindling away; the church was literally falling down; he lived in misery in a hovel, hardly able to find enough money for food, his one consolation the young girl, Marie, who was nominally his servant.

Yet within ten years, he had embarked on rebuilding the church at his own expense, and at building for himself a spacious house in ornamental grounds where he entertained rich and famous people including a cousin of the Austrian emperor.

He offered his guests fine vintage wines. His gardens were filled with monkeys, peacocks and parrots. By early 1917, still greater schemes were on hand. There was no proper road to Rennes-le-Château, so he would build one in order to have a car. He would build a tower over two hundred feet high, to dominate the country around. At this point, he suddenly died, at the age of sixty-five.

Just before his death, he saw an old friend, the priest from a neighbouring village. Everyone agreed that he came away from Saumière looking pale and shaken, and that he never completely recovered from whatever shock he had had.

Did anyone else know what Saumière's secret was? If so, it was probably Marie, who had stayed with him throughout his life, and she dropped hints that she would tell something before she died. This was not until 1953, but nobody knows what she had to tell, for a stroke deprived her of speech, and she struggled in vain to make herself understood. Can we guess what she wanted to say?

The known facts are these. In 1888, Saumière started to do some urgent repairs on the crumbling church, using a small legacy left to the parish. Three years later, he managed to borrow money off the local authority to continue the work. In the course of this, two masons, under Saumière's directions, had to lift up the flat top of the high altar which was supported on two carved pillars dating from Visigothic times. One of the pillars proved to be hollow and hidden inside were three wooden tubes containing rolls of parchment.

For over a year, Saumière tried to make sense of what was written on the parchment. In the end he took them to the Bishop of Carcassonne. The Bishop sent him to Paris, where he consulted experts in both old manuscripts and in cipher.

While in Paris, he struck up a close friendship, to last over many years, with one of the leading opera singers of the day, a woman called Emma Calvé. He visited the Louvre, where he bought reproductions to put on his walls at Rennes-le-Château. They were Saint Anthony the Hermit by Teniers, and a painting by Poussin of shepherds in a landscape. Then he went home, and told his bishop that he had sold the parchments.

Now work started again on the church. This time, Saumière got the men to lift a flagstone in front of the high altar. On the hidden side of it was the carving of a horseman, perhaps a thousand years old, to judge by the style. He then ordered them to dig a deep trench in the place revealed, and sent them out of the church. Before they went, they saw that there were two skeletons in the hole, and also a pot filled with some shining things that Saumière told them were worthless medals.

At this same time, Saumière and Marie used to leave the village daily, with baskets on their backs. They would be seen wandering across the uplands around the village. He explained that they were collecting stones in order to build a grotto in the garden by the cemetery, and so indeed he did.

But why did he spend whole nights shut up in the

cemetery? And why, in the course of that time, should he have effaced the inscription on the tomb of Marie d'Haut-poul, Marchioness of Blanchefort, and great lady of the district just before the French Revolution? When he was challenged, his answers were always evasive.

It was soon after, that he left the village for long periods. When the Bishop or anyone else wrote to him, they received vague replies that he had prepared in advance and that Marie dated and sent off for him.

Then work on decorating the church started, with a group of artists and sculptors recruited from no-one knew where and Saumière himself superintending the work down to the last small detail.

When the church was finished in 1897, the Bishop came to the opening ceremony. He should have rejoiced at so much work done at so little cost to the diocese, but instead he was seized with a strange uneasiness. He may have

remembered the inscription 'Dreadful is that place', for he never went back again.

When a new bishop succeeded, Saumière put off requests to go and see him for over a year. In the end, he went, and was asked where he had obtained his money. Saumière said that it had come from a penitent, as a gift to himself, not the church, and that as he had had the name in the confessional, he could not reveal who it was.

But who, in Rennes-le-Château, had so much money? It was suspected that Saumière might have obtained the money by charging people to say Mass for them, but could that have raised such vast sums? Had Emma Calvé sent it to him? But she was now married.

In 1910, when he was still silent, he was suspended from his duties as priest. It had little effect. All the village crowded into a chapel that he had built himself. The man sent to succeed him preached to an empty church.

One indisputable fact emerges from all this: at some point Saumière had obtained a huge amount of money. This happened after he found the parchments in the high altar. What were they, and who put them there?

We do not have the original parchments, but exact copies of two have survived. They consist of passages from the Gospels, with some letters underlined and some extra letters put in in such a way as to suggest they may be a cipher. Experts have said that the style of writing places them within the last three or four hundred years. They were clearly written by an educated person with a knowledge of the Bible and a knowledge of Latin. Possibly Saumière parted with the originals in exchange for a key to the puzzle.

Who could have written these manuscripts, and who placed them in the tomb? There may be a clue in the symbol ⚭ which appears on one of the parchments. This can also be found on the tomb of Blanche d'Hautpoul, which Saumière took so much trouble to obliterate (in the churchyard). Unknown to him, a copy of it had already been printed, and so we know what it said.

The upright stone gave her name and dates, the flat stone bore some strange inscriptions, such as:

```
E
T
I     RÉDDIS  RÉGIS
N
A     CÈLLIS  ARCIS
✳
PX
```

There is also a formalised drawing of some eight-legged creature. This tombstone is known to be the work of the priest of Rennes-les-Bains at the time of the French Revolution, Antoine Bigou. Does the ⚭ sign mean that he wrote the manuscripts too?

It is on such thin and strange evidence that those who have sought to discover the mystery of Rennes-le-Château have worked. ETINAPX makes no sense, but what is the point of the little cross just before the last two letters? The familiar form of the cross, the Latin cross, has the lowest arm longer than the others. This cross, with four arms of equal length, is known as the *Greek* cross. What if the last two letters are taken as being Greek? This would give ET IN ARKH.

Who Knows?

It sounds like the start of the famous tag, *Et in Arcadia ego: I, too, was in Arcady*, that is, in a pastoral land of perfect happiness. The phrase can be taken to have another meaning: *Even in Arcady, I can be found*, and *I* in this case means Death.

There is a famous painting of shepherds in an idyllic landscape leaning upon a tomb that has these words written upon it.

What is this painting? It is a landscape by Poussin, the very same one which Saumière brought back from the Louvre.

Now comes a yet stranger coincidence. Recently photographs have been taken to show a place which bears an almost uncanny resemblance to the place which Poussin painted over three hundred years ago. It is near to Rennes-le-Château, and it is also near to a village called Arques, pronounced Arc. *I, too, was in Arques?*

What should we make of REDDIS REGIS? Is it Reddae of the King, that is to say, Rennes-le-Château? How about CELLIS ARCIS? *Cella* is a place of concealment, a storage place; *arx* is a castle, a fortress, or is it once again Arques? Then there is the eight-legged creature. Is it an octopus or a spider? In French, this is *araignée*, pronounced rather like *à Rennes*, that is to say, *at Rennes*. What was Bigou saying on this tombstone that Saumière wished to hide?

Not very long after Bigou's death, a picture was placed in the church at Rennes-les-Bains. It shows Jesus lying dead in front of a cave. His arm points towards a tray, under which there is an enormous spider. Suppose these words are put into French. The *spider* is *araignée* again, *at Rennes*. The *tray* is *le plateau: plateau* has another meaning in French as well as in English. *The dead man* in French is *l'homme mort*. *L'homme mort* is the name of a stream which flows on a plateau near Rennes.

It was exactly this sort of punning on place names which Saumière took up in his own church. The devil under the holy water stoup is in a sitting position: a rock in the district is called the Devil's Armchair.

Two of his fingers form a circle: there is a spring called the Circle Spring.

His fingers press down upon his knee: a rock with five hollows in it is known as the Devil's Hand.

One of the paintings shows land which is very *flowery* or *fleuri*: this used to be the land of the Fleury family.

Above all, there is a constant emphasis on caves.

A statue of Saint Anthony the Hermit, the saint of whom Saumière brought back a painting from Paris, reminds us that he is associated with caves. Under the high altar is a picture of Mary Madalene weeping in a cave with a skull nearby. Is this *the dead man* again?

The inscription beneath the picture is taken from one of Saumière's manuscripts, and includes the words MAG-DALENAE LACRYMAS (the tears of the Magdalen). In the district there is a spring, known as the Spring of the Magdalen. Does the shape of the altar suggest a dolmen, a prehistoric tomb, and could this be the cave entrance? It certainly reminds us of something else: the rock shaped like a sepulchre in the place that so closely resembles the Poussin painting.

Once one starts to look closely, do the figures of Christ in the Stations of the Cross suggest a route to follow? In one of them he is crawling, pushing away a big stone. This detail cannot be found in the Gospels. When the soldiers dice for his garments, the dice is made unnaturally big to display the numbers 5 and 7. Is this to give the seeker instructions as to how many steps he must take? As the pictures are examined in detail, more and more hints appear.

What does it all add up to?

From the Middle Ages onwards, there are stories of gold being found near Rennes-le-Château. Bigou had knowledge of something, and it may very well have been he who left the cipher messages in the tomb.

A man called Boudet, who was priest of Rennes-les-Bains while Saumière was at Rennes-le-Château, also suspected something. He wrote a book called *The True Celtic Language and the Cromlech of Rennes-les-Bains*, most copies of which have disappeared. At first sight it seems to consist of crazy guesses at the origin of names, but did he give a clue to some other sense when he wrote of how much the Phoenicians loved puns and hidden meanings? At one point, he talks of a cave used as a store for grain, but the word *blé* has also the slang sense of gold. Under guise of writing about place names, he describes how one may get to some place that itself has no name. It is unreachable in winter, one needs to be warmly dressed, there is water, darkness, and, yet once again, a cave.

Are there more cryptic hints in the churchyard at Rennes-les-Bains on tombstones placed while Boudet was priest which bear inconsistent or sometimes false dates? Yet there is no sign that Boudet acted upon any knowledge he might have had, or that he ever enjoyed any wealth. Nor can we tell if there is any connection at all with the violent murder in 1897 of another priest in the district. No money was taken from him, and there was no apparent motive. Did somebody kill him because he suspected too much?

All we can say is that Saumière, the poor peasant's son,

the banished priest, found some source of enormous wealth. What he found was very probably gold, and to judge by a massive statuette found partially melted down after his death, it seems likely that he, like the coiners of the Middle Ages, melted something down for the value of the metal.

The nearest he ever came to admitting anything was when a friend said jokingly that he had found a treasure. He replied in the local patois, 'I was shown it, I took it, and I keep it.' It would seem, however, that he did not want all knowledge of the treasure to end with his death, because he left a succession of clues in his church.

What could this treasure have been? Was it Roman or Visigothic, did it belong to the Knights Templar? Here, the possible answer is the most astonishing part of this extraordinary story.

In the year A.D. 70 the Roman Emperor, Titus, sacked Jerusalem and bore off the treasure of King Solomon's Temple. It was one of the greatest treasures ever known in the world, and he bore it in triumph to Rome. The Arch of Titus shows pictures of it, such as a slave with a gold candelabrum. Then in 410, when the Goths sacked Rome, they took the treasure away.

At one time, they kept it in Carcassonne, the walled city twenty miles from Rennes-le-Château.

It may well have been for this reason that, during the second World War, the German dictator Adolf Hitler ordered the city to be evacuated, and sent in squads of soldiers to carry out extensive excavations.

Some of the treasure went to Toledo, and part of it was discovered near there in the nineteenth century. Was any of it hidden in France, and if so, is this what Saumière found near Rennes-le-Château? The lame demon near the church doorway – can he be identified with Asmodeus, the legendary guardian of King Solomon's treasure? Is he the key to the mystery?

And the person who nowadays has placed notices at the entrance to the village forbidding all excavations: what does he suspect, or what indeed does he know?

By the Pricking of my Thumbs

Cut a hazel-rod on St John's Eve or Good Friday. Take a twig of mountain ash at midnight on the third day after Lady Day. It must be cut at a crossroads, or, according to some beliefs, it must be cut by a man born under the sign of Libra. Bind the rod to a child who is about to be baptised with the name of John, or the rod itself can be baptised. Give it the name of Caspar if it is intended to search for gold; Balthasar if for silver; and Melchior if for water.

These are just a few of the beliefs that were once widespread in Europe about the ancient art of dowsing, that is, divining the whereabouts of water or metal hidden beneath the ground.

As with many old traditions, dowsing interests two different sets of people. Firstly there are the ones who do it because they have always done it. It is said that in England dowsing is more common in the West Country than anywhere else, because this was the area where it was first introduced. It happened during the reign of Queen Elizabeth I when German miners came to Cornwall to try to find new traces of metal in the old tin mines.

One of the first serious accounts of dowsing in English is

by an eighteenth-century chemist, William Cookworthy of Plymouth, who was convinced that dowsing could be used to trace both different metals and water. A simple form of dowsing is still used by the workmen of the South Western Gas Board, some of whom could well be the descendants of Cornish miners.

A few years ago, the gas supply failed at a Plymouth school, and nobody knew where the main was. The workmen who came to look for it produced two length of thick copper wire, and held them at shoulder level, with both lengths of wire facing forwards. They said that when they reached a spot over the gas main, the metal rods would swing towards one another.

Several frankly incredulous onlookers wanted to try, and to their surprise they found that in certain places the rods moved visibly. In the case of the only woman who tried, the rods moved so violently that they crossed over and hit her on the sides of her neck.

The workmen, sensibly enough, retired to the comparative warmth of their van, while their amateur helpers traced out a line that had one gentle curve and one right angled bend. The men then dug up along the line and revealed the exact course of the gas main, much to the disappointment of all the boys who by now had persuaded themselves that the headmaster was looking for gold.

The most striking feature of the whole business was the matter-of-fact attitude of the gasmen, who took this as a normal, routine way of doing their job.

On the other hand there has been, since the period between the two world wars, a revival of what might be called a little more intellectual interest in dowsing. It is interesting that the people who have concerned themselves with the subject have included several university professors, and, particularly in France, a number of clergy.

In writing about dowsing, they have taken trouble to avoid what might be called an emotional, romantic approach to the subject. There is little about violent, pricking sensations at the base of the thumbs, or about the dowser staggering helplessly because his rod moves so strongly which characterise some accounts of dowsing in fiction. In fact, it is said that if this happens, the dowser must be holding the rod too tensely, or that he is trying to resist its movement when he feels a faint tingling in his thumbs.

Instead, it is stressed that dowsing is a technique that has to be learnt with patience and a great deal of hard work.

One famous French dowser suggested that anybody wishing to learn should first practise over visible objects, because at first nothing would seem to happen and it was only through experience that one learnt how to recognise and then interpret the sensations. He said that anyone wishing to learn how to gauge the depth of water should practise intensively over wells of a known depth.

In general, the emphasis is not that dowsing is an inborn art, but that it is a skill that can be acquired. Some people will have a greater aptitude than others, and some writers have claimed that younger people are better at it than older people.

This of course poses a major question, which is how much firm proof there is that it really works? Not many people have first-hand experience, and most of the books on dowsing seem to be written by the completely converted. What is interesting is the record of individual dowsers.

One man who was prominent in the revival of dowsing was an Army officer, Major C. A. Pogson. Between the wars, when the British ruled India, he was appointed Water-Diviner to the Government of Bombay, his task being to find water for famine relief. In a three-year period, wells were dug at a hundred and thirty sites which he indicated, and water was found at all except two, at or before the depth he predicted. In several others, water was struck but not in sufficient quantities to be of much value.

This gives a hundred and twenty-one successful wells, that is about ninety-three per cent.

On his return to England, Major Pogson continued his work, and detailed records exist of sixteen cases where he worked for such clients as the Middlesex County Council, the Northhampton Brewery and the Co-operative Wholesale Society. Water was found on all the sites he suggested, though in one case it was insufficient and an alternative site he had indicated was then tried with greater success. On two of the sixteen occasions he under-estimated the yield quite considerably.

Twice, in dealing with depths of about two hundred feet he had errors of eight per cent and of ten per cent as to the depth at which water would be found. In one other case, he suggested a depth of three hundred and sixty feet for water. Water was in fact found at three hundred and seventy-four feet, but it was also struck earlier at two hundred and seventy-eight. On this occasion, Pogson thought he had not allowed sufficiently for the effect of a thick band of heavy London clay under the surface. Other than these errors as to yield and depth, his predictions in all these cases proved accurate.

Sceptics may deny that certain people can detect water or metals beneath the ground. Other people may ask by what means do they do it? Three possible explanations have been put forward.

The most obvious is that it is all done, consciously or subconsciously, by observation, and that the dowser is 'reading' the geological structure of the land. Certainly writers on dowsing have stressed that in order to be really successful the dowser must have a knowledge of geology to help him to know in which areas to start looking.

Other factors may give a clue. For example, in dry countries white ants tend to nest over subterranean water, and may tunnel down for fifty or sixty feet to reach it. It is interesting that many dowsers say that their powers are greatly diminished if they are blindfolded, which suggests that observation does play some part in what they are doing. Equally, it could mean that they feel much less confident in walking about blindfold, so cannot concentrate their whole attention on their work.

All writers on dowsing seem to agree that it requires a great deal of concentration, and may leave the dowser feeling exhausted.

The second possibility is that dowsing is done by psychical means. Martin Luther, who as the son of a German miner might have seen dowsing done in his youth, said that it was 'black magic'. Nowadays we would not use such a term, which implies a judgement, but many practising dowsers are convinced that they are working by extra-sensory perception.

Extra-sensory perception, or E.S.P., is grasping something without use of sight, sound, smell, touch or taste, somehow bypassing the normal channels of knowledge. At present, there is considerable interest in the subject, and many controlled experiments have been made. These are often concerned to see if one person can divine what another is thinking and numbers on playing cards or the shape of a design may be used for the experiment. The results seem to indicate that a few people can score a higher rate of success than chance alone might allow.

Another form of spontaneous E.S.P., which many people claim to have experienced, is to think suddenly of a person of whom they are very fond, perhaps in what may prove to be the moment of illness or death.

The President of the British Society of Dowsers, Major-General J. Scott-Elliot, wrote to *The Times* in December 1973 to state his belief 'as a thoroughly practical person' that dowsing is done by E.S.P. Like a number of other dowsers, he takes this belief to what might be called its logical conclusion, that it is not necessary to visit the actual terrain but that preliminary work can be done over a map. In his letter, he claimed to have found three archaeological sites during the year, two in Banffshire and one in Berkshire, having done the preliminary map dowsing in London,

The third possibility is that dowsing has some scientific basis but that we do not at present understand what it is. Television has made all of us unpleasantly familiar with a mechanical process that in some ways resembles dowsing: soldiers with mine detectors looking for explosives. The metal detectors have a more peaceful use in archaeology, and a few years ago they were so popular that the Sunday papers were full of advertisements for them. Archaeologists became worried that amateurs using these detectors might damage sites, and the advertisements stopped, but there are still many complaints that unscrupulous people are using these metal detectors to locate and steal treasure.

This now familiar process raises the question of whether the dowser and his rod are somehow acting as a detector without using any mechanical means.

Does the rod itself have some particular property? There has been a great deal of discussion as to what form it should take. Hazelwood is the most popular, but other woods have been used with apparently equal degrees of success, such as apple, whitethorn, privet and rhododendron. Traditionally, the wood should be forked, and one end of the fork held in either hand, but not all dowsers agree.

Some dowsers prefer quite other substances, such as whalebone. Others use a metal, ranging from the odd bits of copper wire used by the gasmen, to more sophisticated devices acting on a pivot and given such names as the motorscope and the geodetic rod. Some of the French dowsers who have made a great contribution to the subject have not used a rod at all, but preferred a pendulum.

Such a very wide range of substances have been claimed to work that it seems possible that the actual rod itself does nothing: it may only indicate movements on the part of the dowser, made without any conscious thought or will on his part, that otherwise would be invisible.

In other words, it could be the human body itself that is the instrument.

What is the body responding to? It has been suggested that it could be a change in the level of radioactivity at different spots on the earth's surface, or that it might be changes in the earth's magnetic field, caused by what lies underneath the surface.

Those who believe in the physical basis of dowsing think that the human body may be sensitive to such things in the same way that many people claim to know it is going to rain by an ache in an old injury, and others seemed to be affected emotionally by the approach of thunder. One argument in favour of believing that some sort of current is passed into the human body is that a number of dowsers claim to be unable to work if wearing rubber boots or rubber gloves, rubber being an insulating material.

Whatever the truth of the matter may be, it is certainly a subject worth investigating. It could possibly throw some light on our knowledge of the past.

The late Reginald Allender Smith, who was Keeper of the British and Roman Antiquities Department of the British Museum, and Director of the Society of Antiquaries, claimed that at the centre of every prehistoric temple would be found a spot from which a number of underground springs radiated. He called such spots 'blind

springs'. One man, Guy Underwood, was so impressed by this theory that he learnt dowsing in order to investigate it. He decided that blind springs can be found at Stonehenge, Avebury, the stone alignments at Carnac in Brittany and the Erechtheion on the Acropolis at Athens. If this really played a part in the choice of sites, it would suggest that a knowledge of dowsing is very much older than the written records we have of the subject, and that the divining rod

might be the same as the wand which is a very ancient symbol of magic.

More significant is the possible implication for our future. The growth in world population makes the question of growing enough food ever more urgent. To make things worse, there are severe droughts in some parts of the world, such as Africa south of the Sahara. The discovery of new sources of water could transform life for some communities.

It is the custom of the 'developed' nations to think that advanced technology will solve problems, but in certain parts of the world it may be better to offer simple techniques that uneducated people can use for themselves. The traditional craft of dowsing may have something to teach us yet.

Who Stole the Necklace?

'Kill them!' 'Murder!' 'Vengeance!' 'Kill the Austrian woman!' 'We'll take her heart for a stew and her liver to trim our bonnets!'

It was one of the terrifying moments of European history. The mob had learnt how much power it possessed, the power of a group of people welded together in a collective frenzy.

An army of women was escorting the King and Queen of France from Versailles to Paris. They danced round the coach, exulting, and they waved pikes on which were stuck the heads of the slaughtered royal guards. 'Kill them,' they kept on chanting. 'Kill her, the traitress, the murderess, the thief.'

To us, looking back, the French Revolution seems almost inevitable. We see its causes as very deep-rooted: the women who howled round the coach were concerned with more immediate things. Above all, they wanted enough to eat.

Why should the Queen live in luxury at Versailles while they and their children starved? She was, after all, only a depraved woman, a common thief?

On that nightmare journey, which one who rode in it called 'the funeral cortège of monarchy', the Queen must have heard in her ears the taunt, 'What became of the diamond necklace?'

It was useless for her to say that she did not know. The necklace was one of the sparks that had set off the Revolution.

It is a strange story, on a larger-than-life scale. It was played out in Versailles, the greatest of all palaces, designed to glitter and to dazzle. All the images of Versailles are of brightness: the hall of mirrors reflecting and re-reflecting the brilliance of diamonds as the King and courtiers paraded: fountains stretched in a seemingly endless line with their drops sparkling in the sun.

There, in the centre, shone the Queen, Austrian-born Marie Antoinette, with her dazzling complexion, her queenly carriage, her elegance and her grace. Marie Antoinette was not the woman to ask what lay beneath a glittering surface. Wit and learning depressed her, she said, or again, 'I am terrified of being bored.'

The great mass of people in France were completely cut off from this dazzling world, but one who did belong to it was the Cardinal Prince de Rohan. One of the greatest French noblemen and a prince of the church besides, he was a man of charming manners and magnificent presence. A world record shot with his gun, he was also a giver of scandalous parties. His attractive appearance hid overpowering ambition.

Unfortunately for him, his ambition was not being fulfilled. He wished to become the chief minister to King Louis XVI, which, because of the King's sluggish mental abilities, would have made him the supreme power in France. But Marie Antoinette was opposed to him. While he was French ambassador in Vienna, he had ridiculed her mother, the Austrian Empress, and at the same time spread rumours about herself. For this, she refused to forgive him.

The Empress, too, had objected to the Cardinal's way of life. He was ostentatious, outrageous, and what was worse, all the ladies in Vienna were completely bewitched by him. Perhaps they wished to supplant the lady whom at one time he took round Europe with him dressed up as a choir boy. For the Cardinal had some strange associates for a priest. Strangest of all was the so-called Count Cagliostro.

Cagliostro was ageless. He was supposed to have been taught the ancient mysteries of the Temple of Solomon, to have witnessed the Crucifixion. He claimed to have the power to heal the sick, to make diamonds, to turn base metals into gold.

Cagliostro sounds like a charlatan, dressed in his robes covered with occult symbols, burning incense at his candle-lit séances. It is not hard to believe that he may really have been a Sicilian adventurer of great dramatic talent.

And yet there was something a little more than the charlatan about Cagliostro. Perhaps the new popularity of hypnotism at the time can in part explain it. A woman who took a dislike to him said that, nevertheless, it took a tremendous effort of will to withstand him. Otherwise, she said, she would have become his dupe. Certainly Cagliostro, charlatan though he may sound to us, took in the cunning, worldly Cardinal Prince de Rohan.

The last of this strange quartet was the Countess de la Motte-Valois. She bore the name of Valois because she was acknowledged as being a descendant of the French royal family of that name. In spite of this she had known extreme poverty in her youth, and as a child had actually begged in the streets. De la Motte was her husband's name, the 'Countess' was borrowed from another family of de la Mottes who conveniently had a title.

The Countess was in her late twenties, a year younger than the Queen, not beautiful, but with that sort of animation that often makes more impression than beauty. She was a woman in whom the pride of her ancestry and her fierce ambition struggled to overcome her extremely mediocre circumstances, for Monsieur de la Motte had proved to be no richer than she was herself.

In an effort to get money she approached the Grand Almoner of France to ask for a pension so that she would not disgrace the great name of Valois. The Grand Almoner, who happened to be the same unprincipled Cardinal de Rohan, was deeply impressed by her charms. The meeting, and their association, was to lead to a disastrous end for them and for France.

It was in 1784 that the trouble began, when the Countess de la Motte had gone to live in Versailles in hopes of finding someone to help her financially. According to both her own account and to that of the Cardinal, he suggested that she should approach the Queen. Both accounts agree on this (though on very little that follows), that during their discussions the Cardinal admitted that he himself was profoundly distressed because the Queen did not show any favour to him. Now the mystery starts.

What apparently happened is that the Countess became known to the Queen, who took a violent fancy to her. This would not have been altogether surprising, since the Queen's intense, sentimental relationships with some of her women friends were a matter of comment at court.

Partly for fear of antagonising one of these women, the Duchess of Polignac, the Queen could not admit her new friendship openly. However, she arranged that the Countess de la Motte should be allowed free access to her at the Petit Trianon in the grounds of Versailles, which was entirely against the usual strict etiquette of the court.

The Cardinal observed her coming and going late in the evening. He begged her, on these occasions, to put in a good word for him with the Queen.

At first, the Queen would not believe anything good of him. Finally she suggested that the Cardinal should write her an explanation of his earlier behaviour. To his joy, a letter came back on the finest gilt-edged paper: she understood all and was happy that she need no longer consider him guilty.

This was the start of a correspondence that grew warmer and warmer in tone. Then the Queen asked that the Cardinal should raise six thousand francs that she needed for a confidential gift to charity. Later, there came a request for another similar sum. The Cardinal was happy. Oddly enough, at the same time the Countess became visibly richer.

Only one thing continued to distress the Cardinal. In public, the Queen still refused to acknowledge him. The steady flow of letters assured him that this was for reasons of state, but he longed to hear from her own lips that she had really forgiven him.

Then at last, this was arranged. The time was midsummer and it was the Queen's habit to stroll in the grounds of Versailles in the evening. Many people gossiped about these walks, for, as the Emperor of Austria had warned his sister, her lack of care for convention and her ill-chosen friendships were rapidly getting her a bad reputation.

The Queen suggested to the Countess de la Motte that before seeing the Cardinal face to face she would like a chance to observe his behaviour. They agreed that the meeting should take place at night in the gardens with the Queen hidden behind a hedge listening, while another girl played her part.

The idea of substitution probably came from a scene in the very popular play, *The Marriage of Figaro*, which was soon to be even better known as the basis of Mozart's opera.

The Countess managed to find an exceedingly pretty girl, who was at the same time sweet, naïve, and immoral, who agreed to play the part.

The rendezvous was set for a part of the park known as the Grove of Venus. There, hidden behind trellises of green leaves in the dark of night, the Cardinal met what he imagined to be the Queen. There was no beam of moonlight for either to make out the other's face. She gave him a rose, he knelt and kissed the toe of her slipper, then, at a warning of people approaching, he hurried off.

Now that the Queen believed the Cardinal was sure of her favour, she decided to make one final test.

Towards the end of the previous reign, two famous jewellers, Böhmer and Bassenge, had started to make a diamond necklace for the King's favourite, Madame du Barry. It was to be one of the greatest pieces of jewellery in the world. The rows of the necklace and the tassels which hung from it contained no fewer than six hundred and forty-seven diamonds, with a total weight of two thousand eight hundred carats.

Twenty-one of these stones were ten carats or more in weight, and another twenty-three averaged nearly five carats each. It is difficult for anyone who is not a jeweller to envisage what this means, but as a comparison a *one* carat stone, the largest commonly seen in a jeweller's window, is just over six millimetres in diameter. In 1960 a firm of American jewellers estimated the cost of producing a similar necklace to be well over a million pounds. It would cost more today.

The Queen's suggestion was no less than that the Cardinal should negotiate to buy this necklace for her. He at once opened negotiations. The money, an enormous sum of more than one and a half million francs, would be paid by instalments. At one point, he gave the jewellers a note of authorisation signed 'Marie Antoinette de France'.

At last arrangements were concluded and the necklace was ready to be delivered. The Cardinal went to de la Motte's *appartement* in Versailles, and waited there in a room lit only by one small lamp.

Suddenly a voice was heard, 'In the name of the Queen!' He watched while the Countess handed the parcel to a messenger. It was, he thought, the man whom he had seen escorting her away from the Trianon, the man whom she had told him was a trusted servant of the Queen's.

The Cardinal waited. He waited to see the Queen appear in the necklace in public, and he waited for her to send for him as the first stage of his political advancement.

The jewellers waited as well. They were exceedingly anxious to receive the money, and in the end they sent a note to the Queen, saying how happy they were she should have the diamonds and hoping she 'would not forget' the firm which had supplied them. The Queen burnt the letter in the flame of a candle with the remark, 'This is hardly worth keeping.'

As time went on, the Cardinal became more and more

anxious when the Queen did not wear the necklace, but the Countess de la Motte kept on assuring him that she was waiting to have it revalued to see if the price was a fair one. The jewellers were now facing bankruptcy as they had had to borrow so much money to buy the diamonds for the necklace. They approached one of the Queen's ladies, and when she denied all knowledge of the necklace, they finally saw the Queen herself. She told them that she had never seen the necklace in her life.

At this point, the mood changed abruptly to one of shock and panic. The Cardinal was summoned to face the King and Queen and the three chief ministers of the realm. The Cardinal explained how he had bought the necklace on the Queen's behalf, working through the Countess de la Motte. But the Queen denied that she even knew who the Countess was. The jewellers produced their letters of authorisation, but the Queen denied having written them. It was argued that a crowned monarch always signed with the Christian name and that the Queen would never have added 'de France'. Everyone, it was said, ought to know this, at least everyone of the Cardinal's social standing.

The King, spurred on by the Queen, decided to act. As Rohan, in his Cardinal's robes, was walking through the Hall of Mirrors, a voice rang out suddenly, 'Arrest Cardinal Rohan!' At once, he was surrounded. With an amazing air of calm, he bent down as if to adjust a buckle or garter.

In that moment, he scribbled a note behind the shelter of his red cardinal's hat. He managed to slip it to his confidential servant, who rode straight to the Cardinal's house in Paris, and there burnt all the letters from Marie Antoinette. The Cardinal was imprisoned in the Bastille, and a few days later the Countess was taken there too.

From then on, the whole situation turned into a sort of game of truth. In the absence of concrete evidence it appeared impossible to make out who was lying. The Cardinal said that the Countess de la Motte had engineered everything and that he was entirely innocent of the matter. In other words, he was asking everyone to believe that he, a prince, a great churchman who was also one of the chief social figures of the time was as easily taken in as any innocent just up from the provinces.

The Countess of course had a different story to tell. She said that she and the Cardinal alike had been used for his own evil purposes by the magician Cagliostro. She spoke of a 'witches' sabbath' scene, with a young girl, her own niece, in a trance, in which she was threatened with evil unless her husband took the necklace to England to sell the diamonds there.

Finally, the Queen once again denied that she so much as knew the de la Mottes. When she was told that the Countess had been seen on her own private stair, she said that this was a common trick with imposters.

Cardinal de Rohan chose to go for trial. This meant that the public heard all about the Grove of Venus scene and opinion ran strongly against the Queen. Then a priest gave evidence that Madame de la Motte had arranged it all. She promptly retorted that the person really behind it was Cagliostro, who by now had been put in the Bastille as well.

Cagliostro's account of his life, of how he, born a Christian nobleman, had been brought up by Arabs and initiated into the mysteries of the Pyramids, caused a sensation. With their appetite whetted by this, the public next heard the evidence of Mademoiselle d'Oliva who said she had impersonated the Queen in the Grove of Venus.

Thanks partly to her clever lawyer, the public were enchanted by this girl, who combined a career as a prostitute with winsomeness and naïvety.

Opinion turned against the Countess, especially when English jewellers gave evidence that her husband, who had fled to England, was selling diamonds there.

By now the trial had become the sensation not merely of France but of Europe. Books about it, mementoes and engravings sold like hot cakes.

New evidence came when a man called Villette, a close associate of the Countess, admitted to having forged Marie Antoinette's signature on the contract. It was thought that the powerful Rohan family had put pressure on him to do this. He then went further, and admitted to having forged letters from the Queen to the Cardinal, the very existence of which the Cardinal was steadily denying. His evidence seemed likely to sway the case against Madame de la Motte.

Finally, Villette admitted to having been the messenger, supposedly from the Queen, who had received the necklace. To the very end, the Countess protested her innocence, and pointed out the entire lack of written proof.

At last, the verdicts were given. Villette was sentenced to banishment. Mademoiselle d'Oliva, object of much sentimental pity, was acquitted but reprimanded for impersonating the Queen. Cagliostro was aquitted. The Cardinal Prince de Rohan was condemned to make public repentance and to be deprived of all his offices.

The worst punishment fell on the Countess de la Motte. She was condemned to be flogged naked, and branded on both shoulders, both these punishments taking place in public, and then to be imprisoned for life.

There are some events in history after which it is true to

say that 'things were never the same again'. The diamond necklace trial is one of them. Until then, the French monarchy had managed to make many people believe that the King and Queen were beings apart and worthy of special respect and honour. Now it was shown that the Queen was the sort of woman who *might* have ordered a priceless diamond necklace, who *might* have kept midnight assignations, who *might* have indulged in a secret and increas-

ingly intimate correspondence. Why, the French asked themselves, should they suffer to keep a woman like that on the throne?

The sentence against the Countess, who still maintained her innocence, was carried out in front of a large, hysterical crowd. Many people were horrified by the brutality of the punishment, and said that the Queen, by telling the truth, could have spared her.

Then, the year after the Countess was imprisoned, some outside helper contrived her escape and she fled to England. There she published her memoirs, telling in lurid detail of a love affair between the Cardinal and the Queen and quoting his letters to her.

It was these things that were remembered when the French Revolution broke out and the mob surged round the Bastille, and screamed aloud for the 'pleasure mad', the 'spendthrift', the 'bejewelled', the 'harlot' – the Queen of France!

Who was lying? The Paris mob was certain it was the Queen. Accusations against her became more and more obscene, fanned by a new and even more detailed edition of the Countess de la Motte's memoirs.

By this time, the Countess had died in London, where her husband had remained throughout the affair. The Paris court quashed the sentence against her after her death. In 1793, as part of 'the torrent of blood which was to drench France', the King and later the Queen were executed.

This led in turn to another violent swing of feeling, with the Countess being declared the guilty party.

Nowadays, proof is impossible. At some point, perhaps as early as 1792, somebody removed the main evidence, such as the note approving buying the necklace, from the French state archives.

Some questions are still unanswered. Cardinal de Rohan retired to exile across the Rhine, where he lived the life of a simple priest and died in great sanctity. He was a man who in his day had combined the social prestige of a pop star, a multi-millionaire and the Archbishop of Canterbury. Was he really quite such a credulous idiot as he persuaded everybody he was?

And how about Cagliostro? He was one of the leading Freemasons of his day, and Freemasonry, condemned by the Catholic church as a grievous sin, was at that time a revolutionary movement. When Cagliostro left France he published an open letter calling for the Bastille to be razed to the ground. Many nineteenth-century writers saw Cagliostro as the hand that manipulated the whole affair, so as to discredit the monarchy.

We do know something about the necklace itself, for a necklace made of the largest stones was exhibited in the 1950's. It led to a letter in *The Times* from one of the Rohan family.

'The cost of the necklace was paid off in instalments by the Rohan family over a period of nearly a hundred years. . . .

'It brought no material benefit to the family beyond the satisfaction of meeting a debt of honour.'

Can We Believe our Eyes?

They were old men of nineteen and twenty. Old, because the things they had seen and done had wiped their boyhood away completely. Old, because so little lay before them.

In 1916, the expectation of life of a pilot in the Royal Flying Corps, as the R.A.F. was then called, was reckoned to be three weeks. In the first four months of 1917, it was reduced to a fortnight. At nineteen, you needed to live very intensively to pack a lifetime into two weeks. Every minute counted: the moments flying; the moments when you were all getting drunk, and the party grew wilder and wilder; the moments when you lay on your bed and wondered what, in God's name, this war was all about.

The Great War that had begun in 1914 seemed to drag on for ever. Men died: thousand after thousand until they became million after million. Many died trying to get possession of a few square miles of land in northern France and Flanders – land that was so criss-crossed by trenches, so blasted by shell-holes, that it was no longer recognisable.

The soldiers fought battles that were a confusion of blood and the shattering noise of shells, in which the only gain might be a few yards of trenches. Their companions in this nowhere land were rats and lice. Everywhere, there was mud.

Compared with the infantry, the airmen lived in a different world. At that time flying was something entirely outside most people's experience. They were the first group of men in all history ever to fly planes in war.

They arrived at the fighting front with far too little flying experience. Many were hastily trained in what were, all too often, literally 'crash courses'. Some died during this brief training. At one time the need for pilots was so very urgent that they arrived at their squadron after only fifteen or twenty hours' flying experience back in England, perhaps half of it 'solo', or flying without an instructor.

If you were a single-seat 'scout' pilot you were pilot, navigator, gunner and observer combined, with nobody to help you in the strain of making decisions, or to take over if you were injured. And you had no parachute.

Later in the war a satisfactory form of parachute was invented, and artillery observers who went up in balloons at the end of a cable were supplied with them. They saved many lives. But they were not supplied to the pilots. Some pilots complained bitterly of this. Others thought there would be little chance of using them and did not mind. There was a widespread belief among the 'top brass' that, with parachutes, pilots might be tempted to jump rather than fight if they found themselves in a tight corner. So pilots flew in the knowledge that if their plane should catch fire – and it was covered with highly inflammable canvas with a spirit-based paint – they would inevitably burn to death. Unless, of course, they shot themselves first, as some did.

The planes offered little protection against either enemy guns or the elements. Much of the structure was made of wood braced together by wire. The open cockpit had no heater nor oxygen supply. There was, of course, no radio link with the ground or with other machines, and not even a reliable compass. There were no wheel brakes to use on landing.

Such machines flew everywhere: at hedge height and up to twenty thousand feet, where it was bitterly cold and the oil in the guns froze up. The pilots' only protection against the elements was several layers of thick clothing and three pairs of gloves and a padded helmet. At great heights, besides the cold the lack of oxygen affected the pilots' judgement and will and reduced their strength.

Not all the planes were reliable and tractable, or even pleasant to fly. At one time the staple R.F.C. machine was the B.E. (British Experimental) and it was slow and heavy on the controls and hard to arm with a machine gun.

One young pilot, Arthur Gould Lee, who survived the war and in time became an Air Vice Marshal, wrote in later years, 'Men were sent out to face death in aeroplanes that should have been thrown on the scrap heap many months before.' Even the planes with a better reputation, such as the Sopwith Pup and the Camel, were tricky to take off and land, and ultra-sensitive on the controls. The airfield might be a criss-cross of cinder tracks, five yards wide, set in a potato field.

So, the young men set off to fly reconnaissance sorties over the trenches. The desolate nature of the battlefield below was awful. They attacked the trenches and they attacked troops on the move, gun positions and supply points. Above all, they fought German airmen who were trying to do the same thing.

In the air a chivalrous relationship grew up between the young enemies who were set apart from their fellows. They shared the same problems and dangers, which nobody else experienced or was able to understand. There was a kinship between them. But as kinsmen they had to fight, and these scout pilots fought in single combat, one man in a plane against another man in a plane.

On the ground below raged a different battle involving hundreds of thousands of men. But the air battles were more akin to mediaeval jousting, except that they were fought in hideous earnest. The men on both sides were driven by the same deadly impulse which most of them had neither time nor the wish to analyse. They all shared the same terror of plunging, burning, to their death. In the circumstances, there was little hate, and sometimes they even dropped one another news of their enemies' casualties. When the English succeeded in killing the famous German pilot, Boelcke, they dropped a wreath to a brave and chivalrous enemy.

Under these conditions and in this atmosphere it was possible for one side to assume a psychological supremacy over the other. This was what the German air ace, Manfred von Richthofen, managed to achieve. Richthofen was to other first World War airmen what Drake was to sixteenth-century seamen. He was the man everyone talked about, who summed up all the courage and killing power of the rest. He was a Prussian baron who had trained as a cavalry officer and transferred to flying in 1915. Boelcke taught him his simple, basic rules: fly close to your enemy, aim carefully, and fire. Soon Boelcke was naming him as his own obvious successor as champion 'ace'.

Richthofen was fortunate in his opportunities, and he made the most of them. During his period of fame the

Germans had better planes than most that the English or French could muster. They included the Fokker monoplane, the various Albatross planes with which they had many successes, and clumsy though it may look to modern eyes, the Fokker triplane.

With machines like these, Richthofen, then twenty-two years of age, began a remarkable series of victories. He started in September 1916, and within less than ten weeks he had shot down eleven Allied planes. In his eighteenth

successful fight he was in an Albatross D-III, allegedly twenty-five miles an hour faster than anything the Allies had. The upper wing broke in the air. He landed safely, which helped to add to his growing legend. His score mounted, and he had another narrow escape when he was shot down in a fight with five British aircraft, but he was not injured. Is he invincible? people were asking.

Certainly he was a brilliant leader as well as a solo fighter, qualities which do not always go together. On 9th March, 1917, he and four of his men shot down five British planes, while the rest of the German air arm shot down one. On 2nd April, he scored his thirty-third victory. No wonder that the British airmen began to talk, not about fighting the Germans but fighting Richthofen, in exactly the way that the Spaniards had once talked about fighting Drake.

Between March and May 1917, the British lost twelve hundred and seventy aircraft. Seventy-five were shot down in one five-day period of what came to be called 'Bloody April'.

This success spurred Richthofen to new efforts. By the end of June, his personal score had mounted to nearly sixty, and he was busy organising his 'circus'. The Richthofen 'circus' was a mobile formation which could be moved along the front as quickly as it was needed, and it was outstandingly the most successful group of the first World War. One reason for the name 'circus' was that all the planes were painted in different bright colours, whereas the British planes were a uniform chocolate brown for camouflage and attempts to make them look personal were discouraged. Richthofen himself had an all red machine, which gave him his nickname of the Red Baron, or Red Knight.

By April 1918, Richthofen had claimed no fewer than eighty British or French planes shot down. This made him easily the most successful fighting airman on either side in the war. Then on one day, 21st April, a message was received that a red Fokker plane had been shot down. The pilot was at the controls, dead.

Looking back, it is not surprising that Richthofen was killed, only that he defied all the odds and survived for so long. Air experts ever since have been arguing as to how good he really was. In purely technical terms he may well not have been the most brilliant pilot of his generation; in terms of doing his job, which was shooting down enemy planes, he simply outclassed all others. How was he finally killed?

This is a classic case of how hard it is to trust eyewitness accounts. According to one version, he was, at the time of his death, trying to reach his own lines by gliding after his plane had been hit in the engine. According to another, he was chasing a British plane over the lines. The pilot being chased, Lieutenant May, said that a Canadian captain called Roy Brown attacked and shot down the plane while it was on his tail. Brown himself simply reported that, 'I got a long burst into him and he went down vertically.'

But no eyewitness on the ground mentions seeing Brown's plane at all. It was notorious that pilots, especially novices, could miss enemy planes in the air until they were nearly upon them. Could anybody, let alone numbers of people, so miss seeing a plane from the ground?

The opinion of observers from below was that Richthofen was shot down by ground fire. If so, was it an Australian or British battery? If there were two Allied planes so close to a German one why did ground crews risk shooting at that particular moment?

The official awards do nothing to clarify matters. Brown was decorated for shooting Richthofen down, but so were two men in the British battery. Yet one eyewitness told how Richthofen swerved to avoid the British fire, and that it was the Australian guns which hit him.

This was not the end of the confusion. Medical reports suggested that he had been hit by bullets fired on the same level as himself, and that would mean they had come from another plane. Yet, on the day after his death, the commander of the squadron involved is said to have thanked the ground gunners for their intervention, explaining that the guns of both planes had jammed. This, as many British pilots could testify, was far from unusual.

Air experts are still debating as to how exactly Richthofen met his death. More than half a century later, it seems unlikely that any fresh evidence will appear. More recently, there has been another famous case of how hard it is to get clear eyewitness accounts, even immediately after an event. That was when President John F. Kennedy was assassinated in Dallas, Texas in 1963, and the chief reaction was of shock and bewilderment. If we cannot be sure about how things happened when we have living witnesses to tell us about them, and still and moving photographs, how much do we know for certain about the past?

Banquets for the Dead

There are some mysterious peoples from whom we feel completely cut off, either by time or by space. What exactly was Stonehenge? – a meeting place for tribal gatherings and religious ceremonies? Or was it, as has been suggested, built to record and calculate observations about the stars? What are the rows of stones, more than a mile long, in Brittany? They may be the oldest man-built works in existence, but what purpose did they serve? Again, we can only guess, for it is too long ago to know.

Other mysteries come from remoteness in place. It is only two hundred and fifty years since Europeans discovered Easter Island, out in the Pacific. Ever since then, there has been speculation about the gigantic statues there, with vast heads and tiny bodies. The secret may be hidden in the island's 'rongorongo' writing, but most of this has been burnt and nobody alive can read what is left.

Elsewhere in the Pacific are the temples – or is it the city? – or the fortifications? – on the island of Nan Matol. They look like some primitive Venice, but we do not know who built them, any more than we know for certain who built Zimbabwe deep in East Africa.

Distance in time, remoteness in place, means that the chain has been broken. But there is another mysterious people about whom we really know very little, yet might expect to know much. They were called the Etruscans.

The Etruscans did not live on remote islands or deep in forests, but in Italy. Italy is a country about which a great deal is known. Rome was the capital of a great empire, then a very important centre of the Christian religion. Many of the world's greatest artists have lived or worked in Italy. For all these reasons, it has attracted countless visitors for over two thousand years. Yet most of these visitors have completely ignored the Etruscans. It is not even as if they lived in some little-visited part of the country. One Etruscan city was as near to Rome as Croydon is to London. The most remote was roughly the distance from London to Bournemouth.

Nor were they very far removed from us in time. They overlapped with the Rome of the Roman Empire, and about the Romans – their daily lives, their government, their army, everything else – we have detailed records. Even the language we speak contains many Latin words, which have been kept in use till this day. Why are we so completely cut off from the Etruscans?

The first fact to come out is that they have always been rather a mystery, even in their own time. The earliest signs of them appeared in Italy in about the eighth century B.C. But where had they come from? Here the argument starts.

One suggestion is that the Etruscans were in Italy all the time, and were the same as the native inhabitants, known to archaeologists as the Villanovans. Then quite suddenly, for some reason, they produced a much higher level of culture than they had done before. This theory was put forward by a Greek called Dionysius of Halicarnassus, writing at about the time of Christ. It does not explain why remains of the Villanovans should be widespread in central Italy while the Etruscans were concentrated in the west of the country, in between Florence and Rome.

Then there is the possibility that the Etruscans were invaders from somewhere else. If so, where did they come from? One detailed account is given by another Greek writer, Herodotus, who lived in the fifth century B.C.

According to Herodotus, the Etruscans came from Lydia, in what is now Turkey. The country was hit by a famine, and the people needed something to take their minds off their misery. So they invented games, 'dice, knuckle bones and ball games. In fact, they claim to have invented all games of this sort except draughts.' Their system was to eat one day and spend the whole of the next day playing to try to forget how hungry they were.

After eighteen years, they had had enough. They agreed to draw lots and then half the population emigrated. Herodotus says that it was these people who sailed across to Italy and became the Etruscans.

More recently, the argument as to where the Etruscans came from has been revived. German scholars came up with another theory. They said that the Etruscans were northern people who came down into Italy from over the Alps.

There is still no firm agreement, though the most popular theory nowadays is the earliest one, that of Herodotus. There is also the suggestion that the Etruscans were not just one race but a mixture of incomers and the native inhabitants. In any case, it means that there has been a question mark about them from the very beginning.

So the Etruscans, whoever they were, settled in Italy. Soon, they were one of the two great civilisations there. The other belonged to the Greek colonists in the south of the country and Sicily. There was also, set in between the two, a village of wattle and daub huts of no very great importance. The Etruscans called it *Ruma*.

Gradually, Ruma, or Rome, became more important, but largely because of what the Etruscans taught it. From being mud huts, it turned into a city, but the Etruscans built the foundations in the most literal sense, for they are supposed to have been responsible for its great sewers.

They gave it its political institutions too. One of the famous symbols of Roman public life was the double-headed axe. They borrowed this from the Etruscans. Roman senators wore a toga, and the early forms of this came from the Etruscans as well.

In the same way, the Etruscans taught the Romans how to organise and equip an army. The eagles, which we now think of as the sign of the Roman legions, were an Etruscan symbol.

Other debts were the Roman calendar, and the Roman system of using both a family name and a given name.

Then, as so often happens, the pupil turned on the master. By tradition, early Rome is said to have had six kings, and some of these were Etruscans. The last of them, Tarquinius Superbus, or Tarquin the Proud, was thrown out in the sixth century B.C. According to legend, he tried to recapture Rome with the help of the Etruscan Lars Porsena, but the city was saved by Horatius who defended the bridge over the Tiber. His brave fight is the subject of Macaulay's well-known poem.

> Lars Porsena of Clusium
> By the nine gods he swore
> That the great house of Tarquin
> Should suffer wrong no more.

It sounds impressive as poetry, but attempts to sort out what happened in terms of fact are apt to end in confusion. There have been arguments as to whether there was one king of Rome called Tarquin, or two of the same name. Was Lars Porsena really an enemy, or a Roman king himself? Finally did Horatius ever exist? As with so much else to do with the Etruscans, historians give the impression of groping around in a fog.

For, between the fourth and second centuries B.C., the Romans gradually overwhelmed the Etruscans. All the written records we have about them come from other races and not the Etruscans themselves. It is as if the history of Britain had been written by the commander of the Spanish Armada, by Napoleon and then by Hitler, and nothing written by any natives of these islands survived.

What may well have been the best history of the Etruscans was written soon after the birth of Christ by the Roman Emperor Claudius. He consulted the very few people still alive who could read their language. It is tragic that his work should not have survived. For by the time of Christ the Etruscans had disappeared. They had come; and no-one is certain where they had come from; and now, just as mysteriously, they had gone.

Of course, people, that is to say individuals, do not simply disappear. If there had been gigantic massacres, some word of it would have come down. Even nowadays we know how the Romans set out to destroy the city of Carthage. But the identity of the Etruscans disappeared. Europe has always been full of minorities who have kept their languages and their customs in the face of more powerful neighbours. The Etruscans completely lost theirs in a very few generations.

Nor did their cities survive. There are cities which we know existed, because they were powerful enough to mint their own coinage, but nobody has yet managed so much as to find out where they were.

For a very long time, no-one bothered to wonder what had happened to the Etruscans. For one and a half thousand years, it was as if they had never existed at all. The first sign of any interest in them was in the fifteenth century, when a Dominican friar found inscriptions in Italy in some mysterious ancient language that was neither Latin nor Greek. Was it Etruscan, and if so, what did the inscriptions mean?

Serious interest in them did not, however, begin until the eighteenth century. Then it was not for reasons of scholarship. The people of Rome and other cities suddenly realised that, in the deserted countryside, there were literally thousands of graves. The graves were in the form of underground houses, and were filled with jewels, statues and pottery. The hunt began, and naturally enough, landowners and peasants joined in.

The results were disastrous. Grave after grave was plundered for what could be found inside. One of the worst offenders was Napoleon's brother, who owned the site of an Etruscan cemetery. He acquired thousands of bronzes and vases, and loaded his wife with Etruscan jewels which caused a sensation when she appeared in public. Other items were given away, and many, which seemed less interesting, were simply smashed.

Later, more Etruscan work was destroyed to help keep up the market price of the rest. The tombs themselves were gutted by people who had no understanding of what they were doing, and who had no idea at all who the Etruscans were. No records were kept. What we know about the

Etruscans is in spite of, and certainly not because of, these treasure hunters.

Then, in the middle of the last century, came the man who, more than anyone else, made the Etruscans known. His name was George Dennis. Like his contemporary, Schliemann, who discovered Troy and Mycenae, he was an example of someone who left school young and was largely self-taught. He wrote a book called *The Cities and Cemeteries of Etruria* which is still the leading English work on the subject. Unlike many works of the kind, it gives a sense that Dennis really enjoyed what he was doing, and this still comes across to the reader after more than a hundred years.

Cities and *cemeteries*. At first sight, it seems an odd title. In fact, it sums up the situation exactly, for so many Etruscan cities have disappeared. Roman historians said that there was an Etruscan league consisting of twelve cities: but what cities were they? A few places in modern Italy are known to be on Etruscan sites, such as the university city of Perugia and the cathedral city of Orvieto. There are some other Etruscan cities of which the whereabouts is known, but the sites are completely deserted. Then there are others, such as Caletra, which are a name but no more.

If the 'cities' are an enigma, this leaves the 'cemeteries'. What do they tell us about the Etruscans? The answer is everything and nothing at the same time.

Many Etruscan cemeteries are in remote places, set in some of the most picturesque country in Europe. The tombs are like houses, that are built underground or set into the faces of rocky cliffs.

The walls of these tombs are often covered with very life-like paintings. A favourite scene is a banquet. Husband and wife recline together to eat. This is something that neither the Greeks or the Romans, who segregated women on social occasions, would have allowed. Sometimes their children are sitting beside them, or a dog is waiting hopefully at the foot of the couch.

The banquet scenes are enlivened by music and dancing. Then there are paintings showing the slaves preparing the banquet. They too have music played to lighten their task. In fact, it appears that the Etruscans enjoyed background

music on a scale not known again until the transistor radio was invented.

Other pictures show games and sports: chariot racing, running. Even boxers are shown as fighting to the sound of the flute.

Then there are the objects hidden inside the tomb. There are statues of the dead people. Some show husband and wife together, which suggests an emphasis on the

married state that is rare in the ancient world. There are pottery models of Etruscan houses and temples, and small bronze statues. Many of these are of figures with very long-drawn-out limbs, that look like the work of some modern sculptors. There are mirrors, with scenes engraved on the back, and there is jewellery.

Anybody who is familiar with Greek art will see resemblances between it and some of the Etruscan work, which suggests that there was continuous contact between the Etruscans and Greece. In particular, some of the statues resemble early Greek art, such as the god from the temple at Veii, who has a curved enigmatic smile.

Yet the more one looks at Etruscan art, the more its very individual nature appears. It is very lively. It has an air of what would be, in an animal, a pricking up of the ears. Even in the depths of the tomb, there is an extraordinary sense of enhanced well-being.

As for the men and women in the paintings and statues, they are not merely types, they are individuals, with personal relationships between them. Somebody who was tired of all the arguments about where the Etruscans came from and where they went to, recognised this life-giving quality of Etruscan art. It was D. H. Lawrence, the famous novelist, who protested, 'The Etruscans are not a theory or a thesis. If they are anything, they are an *experience*.'

So, for a moment, we may feel able to share in the Etruscan feeling for life, as if caught up in the soundless noise of their music. Yet we still get back to the point that, in terms of hard fact, we really know remarkably little about them.

For example, what did they believe in? We do know that many of their gods had names corresponding to Greek and Roman gods, such as Uni for Juno, and Apulu or Aplu for Apollo. We know that they foretold the future by the extraordinary method of examining sheep's livers. There are many scenes showing this on the back of mirrors. There is also a bronze model of a liver, labelled to show how different gods influenced different parts of it. This was probably used for training priests to foresee the future.

We also know from their art that they believed in a horrifying underworld figure called Charon. He has a club to crush the skulls of the dying.

The impression that all this gives is that the Etruscans were a fatalistic people. They seem to have accepted what was pre-ordained for them, rather than questioned why things should happen in the way that the Greeks did.

But this is only a surmise. We cannot be certain what the Etruscans thought. In one extremely important way, we are completely cut off from them. The Etruscans had writing, but nobody is able to read what they wrote.

In all, about ten thousand Etruscan inscriptions are known. Very few of these have more than thirty words. One of the few long texts was found by the famous nineteenth-century explorer and writer, Sir Richard Burton. It was found in the most extraordinary way, wrapped round an Egyptian mummy. It was not even in Egypt, but in the country now called Yugoslavia. Not surprisingly, it was not until some time later that the language was identified as Etruscan.

To look at Etruscan writing for the first time is likely to produce feelings of bewilderment. Here is a typical inscription from a tomb.

ƎꙄΑꟼƎꟻ:ИΑꟽ↗:ꟼΑOИꟼΑ:ꟄVꟁWVꟁ:ꙄꟼΑꟼ

Some people may react to this by holding it up to a

mirror, and they would be on the right lines. The language, in fact, was written from right to left. If we look at it the way round we are accustomed to seeing things, the inscription becomes:

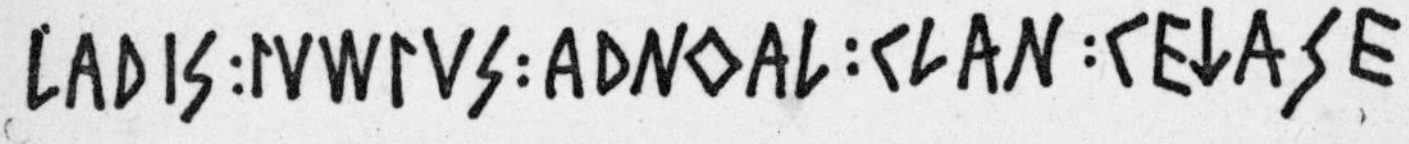

ᒪᗅᗪ I � : I ᘁ W ᒋ ᐯ � : ᗅ ᗪ ᘉ ᗝ ᗅ ᒪ : ᑕ ᒪ ᗅ � : ᒋ ᕮ ᒌ ᗅ ⊅ ᕦ

A number of these letters are recognisable as the Roman form of letters we use ourselves. Others can be identified by anyone who knows the early forms of the Greek alphabet. Lucky, there are enough Etruscan inscriptions for the mystery of the alphabet to have been cracked, and we know now that it was a link between the Greek alphabet and the Roman. This particular inscription reads:

LARIS: PUMPUS: ARNTHAL: CLAN: CECHASE

What in the world does it mean?

We know that the word *clan* means *son*, because it so often occurs in inscriptions. There is also a regular use of the ending *-al*, meaning *of*. The inscription is therefore about *Laris Pumpus the son of Arnth*. As to what *cechase* may mean, nobody knows at all.

One reaction to this inscription may be that Arnth is a very strange name. So are other Etruscan names, such as Pevthi, Vel and Aule. No modern child would be likely to have such names, though he might well have a name that goes even further back in time. There are plenty of Old Testament names still in use, such as Daniel, Joseph and Rachel, as well as classical names like Helen and Julia. The fact that the Etruscan names sound so very unfamiliar all shows the complete lack of continuity between them and us.

Another odd thing is that names such as Pevthi and Vel do not even sound like any other known language. They do not sound like French or Italian or Spanish, all of which belong to the Latin family of languages. On the other hand, they do not sound much like the Germanic languages either, that is German, Dutch, the Scandinavian languages, or that large part of the English language that came from Anglo-Saxon.

For most languages in ancient and modern Europe have a recognisable family tree. There are very few languages which exist in isolation, not related to any others. One of these few is Basque, which is spoken around the Pyrenees. Another 'odd man out' is Etruscan.

So it is impossible to decipher Etruscan by relating it to any other language. It is true that efforts have been made to show it resembles Irish, Finnish and Albanian, among other languages, but none of these suggestions has ever been widely accepted.

So far, there are only about one hundred words in Etruscan which have an agreed meaning. Some of these, such as *clan*, are known because of their context. Others are given a meaning in the writings of Roman authors.

Scholars pore over Etruscan texts in the hopes that if they find the same word often enough its meaning will become clear. But the extent of the problem is shown by a pair of dice, that bear six words on their sides. Presumably these are the number of one to six. It is likely, according to the common arrangement of dice, that the numbers on opposite sides would add up to seven. So *mach* and *zal* may make seven. So would *thu* and *huth*, so would *ci* and *sa*. But nobody has yet proved for certain which of those numbers means *one*, let alone the remaining numbers.

Who Knows?

There is still the hope of a breakthrough in understanding Etruscan. The easiest way would, of course, be to find an inscription with the identical text in Etruscan and some known language, such as Latin. No-one could read Egyptian hieroglyphics until the Rosetta stone was found, which has one version of the text in Greek. An inscription like this, perhaps a plaque in a public place, may yet be found.

The other possibility is, of course, sheer human inspiration. One of the mysteries of the ancient world used to be a script called Linear B. This was thought to be a Minoan, that is a Cretan language, until a brilliant young man called Michael Ventris found that though the script itself was unfamiliar the actual language written in it was early Greek. Tragically, Ventris died young in a road accident. Otherwise, it has been suggested that he, if anyone, might have solved the mystery of Etruscan.

Can we understand more about the Etruscans without knowing their language? There is still the possibility of archaeological discoveries more important than anything uncovered yet. Even after so many graves have been robbed and destroyed thousands of others remain. Some have been shown up by aerial photographs, including photographs taken by the R.A.F. during the war for quite different reconnaissance purposes.

The use of metal detectors also helps in finding underground tombs. So does a type of periscope that can be pushed down into a tomb. Photographs can be taken, and it is then possible to decide if it is worth excavating the tomb or not.

The trouble is that the scientific methods which are available to archaeologists are available to tomb robbers as well. Antiques and works of art are fetching such high prices at present that there is an active black market in Etruscan works.

Another danger is deep ploughing with modern tractors that destroy very much more than the feet of oxen ever did. Then, too, the building of motorways rips through the landscape. As always, it is the developers who have the money to spare, not the archaeologists. It may be that it would be better to concentrate more on excavating Etruscan cities, and not just their tombs. This might cast new light on them, and on other ancient people as well.

From other points of view, there may be a certain value in the fact that the Etruscans can still keep their mystery, not in some distant backwater but in the heart of industrialised and computerised Europe today.

A Malady in the Blood

A high-spirited little boy who is not allowed to play as other boys play because of a fear that if he does he may not live to grow up. A kind, well-meaning father, a mother who is intolerably tense from the strain of seeing her child suffer. It is, tragically, a situation that has happened in many families. Obviously, the father finds it hard at times to carry on with his job, in the factory, shop or office or wherever he works. But what when the father is the ruler of the largest country on earth?

Not merely the ruler, but the absolute ruler as well. The revolutions and struggles which had taken away the powers of the kings of England and France had left Russia untouched. The Czar was called the Father of all his people, a hundred and thirty million of them, who lived in an Empire which stretched from the Baltic to the Pacific, from the Arctic down to the mountains of Afghanistan.

In other words the Czar was an autocrat, a man who rules on his own. A political genius might have managed this unwieldy empire, but Nicholas II of Russia was no politician at all. When he succeeded in 1894 he exclaimed, 'I am not prepared to be a Czar, I never wanted to become one. I know nothing of the business of ruling.'

As a man, Nicholas was affectionate, considerate, at times very gentle. In his appearance, he bore a strong resemblance to his cousin King George V of England. Their mothers were sisters, and the two were sometimes mistaken for one another. In fact, if Nicholas had been the King of England he might have made a popular constitutional monarch.

This relationship between them was typical of the royal families of Europe which still mainly married between one another. The old Queen of England, Victoria, had so many royal descendants that she was known as 'the grandmother of Europe'. It was one of her granddaughters, a German princess, whom Nicholas married less than a month after he became Czar. Once again, on a personal level, the marriage was outstandingly happy. For the rest of his life, Nicholas was completely devoted to 'Sunny', as he called her. It was tragic that she should have played such a part in his downfall.

The Czarina, Empress Alexandra, showed almost from the start that she was unable to come to terms with Russia. This was sad, for in her way she loved the country deeply, and was a sincere convert to the Russian Orthodox faith. On the one hand, she could not understand the fashionable society of St Petersburg, now called Leningrad, which was the capital city. It was as scintillating, as lavish and extravagant as the jewels made by the court jeweller Fabergé, while the Russian drama and ballet were producing some of the greatest works of modern times.

But the German princess was a provincial. She was very shy, and mistrusted brilliant society. The Imperial family withdrew into themselves, and their own way of life was simple. In a large palace, surrounded by armies of servants, the Czar ate plain Russian food and his children slept on camp beds.

Unfortunately, the Empress had no better understanding of another side of Russia. This was the world of the moderate politicians, who sought to give Russia a more broadly based government, with less power in the hands of the Czar alone. She was determined to resist them. 'Be the master and lord, you are the autocrat,' she was to write to her husband. The position she was creating for her family was one of great isolation. To make matters far worse was something quite unsuspected, a secret she carried hidden within herself. Alexandra was a transmitter of haemophilia, a 'carrier'.

Haemophilia is a condition in which the blood does not clot as it does with a normal person, so that bleeding, once started, can go on and on. A minor nose bleed can turn into a disastrous haemorrhage, or bleeding under the skin can cause agonising swelling. It is a sex-linked disease, in that woman can transmit it to their sons and, as carriers but not sufferers, to their daughters. Its origins go far back into history and it is not fully understood today.

It was once called 'the royal disease', because of the way it affected the descendants of Queen Victoria.

Her own youngest son was a haemophiliac, and two of her five daughters were carriers. They in turn transmitted the defective gene to their own daughters, and between them these princesses had at least eight male descendants who suffered from the disease. They included the heirs to the throne of Spain. They also included Alexis, Nicholas's and Alexandra's fifth and last child, and their only son. In a country where women were no longer allowed to succeed to the throne, he was the longed-for future Czar.

Alexis was only a baby when the first symptoms appeared. Oddly enough, although the disease was well known by doctors, the royal families of Europe seemed unaware of how the trouble arose. It has been cited as a gulf between them and reality. His parents decided to keep any hint of Alexis's disease from the Russian people. This was made easier by the isolation, now greater than ever, in which the Imperial family lived.

When Alexis was well and appeared in public, he seemed a lively and very attractive small boy. He had all the normal tastes of small boys, and liked to run, jump, and take risks. Then a knock would cause bleeding into a joint. Soon he would be in almost unendurable pain, from which his only relief was to faint. He might be in a high fever for weeks. So intense was the secrecy with which his disease was surrounded that most of their own household did not understand what was wrong, still less did anybody outside. The Russians, who are often warmhearted, might have sympathised with his parents, but as it was they resented the way in which the family withdrew from outside contacts. Into this situation came, like a charge of dynamite, Gregory Rasputin.

Rasputin, unfortunately, was just what Alexandra imagined a genuine, simple Russian peasant was like. Here at last, she thought, was the warm, passionate, deeply religious soul of Russia : a far remove from the dazzling brilliance of St Petersburg, or the worries of politicians who prated about reform. He was a Siberian peasant who first appeared in St Petersburg in 1905. At that time he dressed like a peasant in loose blouses and baggy trousers, his hair, hands and beard were filthy. He ate his favourite fish soup with his hands, and the French Ambassador said he smelt like a goat.

Who Knows?

It is astonishing that such a man should have been not merely accepted but welcomed into society, but Rasputin had the reputation of being a man of God, and the Russians, like the Indians, had a traditional reverence for holy men. Rasputin certainly had an aura of holiness; he saw mystical visions, he had a great gift for preaching, he had walked two thousand miles on a pilgrimage. His name 'Rasputin' was a nickname given to him in his youth, and means 'dissolute'. At first, women found him interesting as a reformed seducer. It then quickly became obvious that he had not reformed in the least, but it was surprising how many nobly-born women seemed perfectly happy to put up with the smell.

This then was the man who was introduced into the Czar's household. From the beginning, Alexandra saw only one side of him, the Man of God. Any references to his drunkenness, to his dealings with women, she dismissed as slanders. She was too innocent to realise that many people took it for granted she was simply another of Rasputin's women herself.

It is a situation that does not begin to make sense unless one accepts that Rasputin, whatever else he was, was a quite extraordinary person. When he chose, he could have an almost hypnotic effect on people. Nearly everyone who saw him commented on the remarkable quality of his eyes, and this is evident even in the photographs of him.

In other circumstances, Alexandra's interest in Rasputin might have been dismissed as an eccentricity. Most royal persons have hobbies, such as horses or collecting stamps, and two monarchs this century have been recognised as experts on archaeology and marine life. Generally, their subjects appreciate this as it makes royalty seem more human.

Rasputin as a hobby was a rather different matter. In fact, many people began to wonder if he was merely a diversion, or whether 'Our Friend' as Alexandra called him, was threatening to become the effective ruler of Russia. He influenced Alexandra, she influenced her husband.

The reason for his control over her was his effect on Alexis, the young heir to the throne. Here one enters the realm of the inexplicable. Alexis's attacks of haemophilia were not only acutely painful but carried a serious risk that he would die. His parents were obviously profoundly distressed, both because they were kind, loving parents, and because the boy was the heir to a great empire.

On one occasion, when he was eight, Alexis bled for eleven days, until his joints and his abdomen were so filled with blood that his whole body was contorted. The doctors denied him pain-killing drugs for fear of causing addiction. When he was conscious, he screamed and screamed. All through this time, Alexandra remained by his side watching her child suffer.

At the point when everyone was prepared for his death, Alexandra sent a telegram to Rasputin in Siberia and asked him to pray for her son. The reply came back: 'Do not grieve. The Little One will not die.' Next morning, Alexandra was quite serene. 'I received a telegram from Father Gregory and he reassured me completely,' she said. A day later, the bleeding stopped.

Nobody knows for certain on how many more occasions Rasputin intervened when the boy seemed to be bleeding to death. Still less does anybody know how he did it. But all accounts from inside the palace suggest that there were several times when Rasputin stopped the boy's bleeding; not by doing anything, not even by touching him, but simply by being there. How he did so is a mystery.

One suggestion is that he used a form of hypnosis, which caused the arteries to contract. Another is that by calming the child's mother he passed on confidence to Alexis himself. His presence was far more reassuring than constant examination by terrified doctors.

In either of these cases, Rasputin's power is of great

interest to those who study the relation of mind and body. The third explanation is that he was a fraud, who never appeared until some accomplice in the Palace told him that the bleeding was likely to stop spontaneously.

What matters most is not how he did it, but that Alexandra believed he had some supernatural power. She had absolute faith in him, and her love for her son made her more and more dependent on him. She had a kind, affectionate husband who found it painfully difficult to make up his own mind. Small wonder that everyone was starting to ask who really governed Russia: the Czar, his German-born wife, or a drunken, dissolute man whom Alexandra thought was a saint?

The matter was becoming exceedingly urgent, for Russia, together with England and France, was now at war with the German and Austrian empires, in what we know as the first World War. Russia was doing badly. By 1916, there was the almost incredible situation that Nicholas had taken command of the Army while Alexandra ruled at home. She was determined at all costs to keep absolute power in the hands of the family, and to hand on a 'strong country to Baby', for so she still called poor Alexis. In practice, she had Rasputin as an adviser, and she judged everyone else by their attitude to Rasputin. Not surprisingly, a group of Russians decided that the one hope for their country was for Rasputin to go.

The leaders of this group were not politicians or intellectuals, but Russian aristocrats. Among them was Prince Felix Yussoupov, one of the wealthiest men in Russia, whose mother was the Czar's first cousin. Had Rasputin some foreknowledge of what was to happen? Towards the end of December 1916, he produced an extraordinary letter.

'I feel that I shall leave life before 1st January. . . . If I am killed by common assassins, and especially by my brothers, the Russian peasants, you, Czar of Russia, have nothing to fear. . . . Czar of the land of Russia, if you hear the sound of the bell which will tell you that Gregory has been killed, you must know this: if it was your relations who have wrought my death then no-one of your family, that is to say, none of your children or relations, will remain alive for more than two years. They will be killed by the Russian people.'

Two weeks later, Rasputin went to visit Yussoupov at his palace in the capital. Yussoupov received him in a room in the cellars, well furnished with ancient embroideries, carved chairs and a bearskin rug. There, in one of the strangest scenes in history, he fed him with fancy cakes and glasses of wine. Overhead, an early gramophone ground out '*Yankee Doodle Dandy*', while Yussoupov himself sang to a guitar. An hour went past, then another, and Yussoupov could not believe what was happening. Each of the cakes Rasputin had eaten, each of the glasses of wine, had been filled with enough cyanide to poison several men.

After two and a half hours, Yussoupov's nerves could bear no more. He slipped upstairs to fetch a revolver, commanded Rasputin to look at an ornate Italian crucifix, and then shot him in the back. Rasputin fell on the bearskin, and a doctor, who was in the conspiracy, hurried down and pronounced him dead.

Then . . . the 'dead' man rose up. He lunged at Yussoupov, who managed to run away. Rasputin followed him up the stairs, shouting furiously. He ran across the courtyard towards the street, leaving a trail of blood in the snow. The conspirators shot at him again and again, and the last shot hit him in the head. They kicked him, he tried to rise. At last, they overpowered him with blows of a club. They bound him, wrapped him up in a curtain, and managed to thrust him through an ice hole until he disappeared into the frozen river Neva.

It was three days before the body was found. Incredibly, he had managed to free one of his arms from the bonds while he was under the ice. He had died, not of enough poison to kill many men several times over, not of at least two bullets in his body and one in his head, not of the blows aimed at him, but simply of drowning.

Undoubtedly Rasputin was a man of extraordinary power. Many people were convinced he was evil, the Empress saw him as holy. Where did his power come from, and how did he exercise it? What did he really do to Alexis, why did he take so long to die? Nobody has provided a full answer, and so he remains one of the most mysterious characters in all history.

His letter was to prove true. In 1917, at the end of a terrible winter, starving, in the chaos of war, the Russian people rose up against their rulers and forced the Czar to abdicate. At first the new head of government was a man called Kerensky, the sort of politician with whom Nicholas might in the past have made a compromise. Then events gathered momentum like an avalanche that slides down a mountain side. Kerensky was overthrown by Lenin and the Bolsheviks, and the state we now know as Soviet Russia was born. The Imperial family was taken away to Siberia, ostensibly for their own safety. Alexis, who had had a severe haemorrhage, was unable to walk. They spent the winter in a house in Ekaterinburg under close arrest.

Then in the summer of 1918 something happened. What was it? The London *Times* for 22nd July was mainly interested in the news of Allied advances across the Marne.

But it also announced that it had received a report that the Czar had been shot for his part in a counter revolutionary plot. His wife and son had been taken to a place of safety. There was no editorial comment, and a non-committal obituary notice spoke of 'that painful lack of decision that had characterised him from youth upwards'.

A few days later, seven lines of small print reported that Alexis had died of exposure soon after his father's death. The English Court went into mourning, and King George V, the Czar's cousin, and the Queen Mother, his aunt, attended a requiem. For the rest of his life, the King was to reproach himself for not having over-ruled his Prime Minister, David Lloyd George, who advised him not to offer the Czar asylum.

The Times gave it all much less attention than the news of the fighting. When more news did come from Russia, and much of it, oddly enough, was taken from German

newspapers, it was not of the Czar at all. There seemed to be a complete collapse of all normal life: there was violence, hunger, massacres, bound corpses were washed up on the shores of the Baltic. No-one in Russia knew what was happening on the outer world. Even after four years of mass slaughter, the people of Western Europe could still be shaken at news of the total breakdown of law and order.

But what had become of the Czar? In April 1919, his mother left the Crimea on board a British warship. She was gay and discounted all 'rumours' that her son had been killed, and continued to do so until her death nine years later. Why should she behave like this? Partly it was a faith in family solidarity. Not only was Nicholas a cousin of King George V of England, but the German Kaiser William was first cousin to Alexandra, both being grandchildren of Queen Victoria. Some people believed that, before the defeat of Germany, the Kaiser had arranged for the family to be released. A great many more believed that the British Government had spirited them away.

The situation in Russia was so confused that in January 1919, the sympathisers of the Czar were able to send an investigator called Solokov to Ekaterinburg. He thought it possible that the statement by the Bolsheviks was deliberately misleading, and that the Imperial family could have left Ekaterinburg about three weeks before the supposed date of the Czar's death. At the time, the Bolsheviks were saying that it was 'not to be excluded that they escaped'.

Certainly, Solokov found no signs of bodies. What he did find, down a mine shaft, were belt buckles belonging to the Czar and Alexis; an emerald cross belonging to Alexandra; six sets of woman's corsets; and an odd little assortment of metal objects which Alexis's tutor identified as the sort of thing that the boy of thirteen used to carry around in his pocket.

A year later, the Russian Government said that the entire family had been shot, but disclaimed responsibility for it. On the other hand, Trotsky, one of the revolutionary leaders, said that Lenin himself had decided to kill the whole family so that no-one was left for their supporters to rally around.

This has led to the generally accepted picture of what happened. The Czar, his wife, and their five children are thought to have been shot in the cellars of what was renamed the House of Special Purpose. The bodies were then cut up, burned, and the larger bones destroyed by sulphuric acid. Why, if this is true, should such extreme steps have been taken to destroy all remains? The answer may be in the way that the Russians traditionally venerate the bodies of the dead. Nicholas's own father lay in an open coffin for seventeen days while thousands of people filed past him. The Russian leader Lenin still lies embalmed for all to see in Red Square in Moscow today.

The controversy has not ended. It was reopened in 1972 when the first English translation of Solokov's investigation was published. Thomas Preston, who was British Consul in Ekaterinburg in 1918, wrote to *The Times* to say a telegram had been sent to Moscow to say, 'All members of the Russian Royal Family shared the fate of the Czar,' and a copy had been left by mistake in the Ekaterinburg telegraph office. He himself thought that the failure of the family to get in touch with any relations was proof that they all were dead. This belief is shared by the Grand Duke Vladimir, now considered to be the surviving head of the family, and by Earl Mountbatten of Burma, whose mother was Alexandra's sister.

Who Knows?

Or did one of them escape? For many years there were rumours that the youngest girl, Anastasia, was left for dead and then rescued, severely wounded. A number of women have claimed to be Anastasia herself. The most famous was a German, who lived for many years in poverty under the name of Anna Anderson, and struggled to have her claims recognised. Could there be any foundation of fact behind the various stories?

They were such an ordinary family in themselves to have been involved in so much terror and so much mystery. One question is completely unanswered. We do not know the nature of Rasputin's influence on Alexis. But if Alexis had been a perfectly healthy boy would the history of the modern world have been any different?

Paper Boats and Flying Saucers

Two of the most remarkable conquests in history took place within just over ten years of each other, when, almost incredibly, a few hundred men overthrew two powerful civilisations. They were the Spanish conquests of Mexico and Peru.

The Spaniards had first reached the Americas in 1492 when Columbus landed in the West Indies and explored the islands of Cuba and Haiti. From there, it was only a short step to the mainland of Central America. A number of expeditions landed, and returned with crudely made gold ornaments and stories about stone pyramids which led them to name one place Great Cairo. Then a man called Hernan Cortes, mayor of the new capital of Cuba, set off and landed on the coast of what is now Mexico a few days before Easter, 1519.

The Indians were fascinated by his ships, with their high sterns, and their flags and streaming pennants. Two things filled them with great amazement: the horses, which they had never seen before, and the cannon. Cortes set the horses prancing, with bells on their harness, and fired the cannon. When the Indians brought him greetings from Montezuma their leader, he suggested that Montezuma should send him gold.

The gold came and astonished the Spaniards. Their first contacts with the American Indians had led them to assume they were dealing with savages. Here, however, was a gold disc as big as a cartwheel; two gold rods twenty inches long; finely made ornaments shaped like animals; pendants and necklaces.

Montezuma himself refused to meet them, and they waited for more than three months, uncertain what to do. Cortes was encouraged by finding that the people of the coast, who had only recently come under Montezuma's power, were hostile to their new ruler. In the end he sank his ships, so that his men could not retreat, and advanced inland.

He had some four hundred Spanish soldiers, fifteen horses and six guns. Between forty and a hundred local chieftains went with him, as well as natives to carry his stores. They marched through high country, going for three days through desert without anything to drink. When they came to a city called Tlaxcala they met with their first resistance, but thanks to the cannon and horses they overcame an army of what they claimed was more than a hundred thousand men. They marched on and crossed over a pass between two giant volcanoes of over seventeen thousand feet, that were crowned with plumes of smoke though the sides were covered with snow. Their goal was Montezuma's capital, Tenochtitlan, or as it is now called, Mexico City.

Two surprises were in store for them. The first was the city itself. Tenochtitlan lay on islands in a lake, most of which has since been drained, and was joined to the land by a causeway over five miles long and wide enough for eight horsemen to ride abreast. As they approached, they could see huge temples; houses for thousands of people; wide, straight, stone streets.

So far from being backward or primitive, this place looked as splendid as anything to be found in Europe. Montezuma himself, when he came, was a dazzle of gold and silver and glimmering green feathers from some exotic bird. His words of greeting provided the second cause of surprise.

'Our lord, you are weary. The journey has tired you, but now you have arrived on the earth. You have come to your city, Mexico.... This was foretold by the kings who governed your city, and now it has taken place. You have come back to us: you have come down from the sky.'

Cortes did not know what to make of the situation. He was in a magnificent city surrounded by gold and silver work of remarkable skill. Yet steel was unknown, and the sharpest cutting edge was volcanic obsidian. It was the centre of a complicated administrative and legal system that stretched across Mexico, yet all communication was by men running over the mountains. Not only were there no horses but there were no beasts of burden at all, for which reason, perhaps, the people had never made any use of the wheel.

Montezuma had greeted him courteously, indeed with surprising eagerness, but Cortes must have wondered what lay beneath the surface. Already he had seen many signs that the people of Mexico, the Aztecs, practised human sacrifices. This had reached its peak when a great temple was dedicated with twenty thousand victims killed in a space of six days. It was among these people that the Spaniards were isolated, their only escape route a long causeway.

Who Knows?

What happened was an extraordinary process of psychological warfare, between Montezuma and Cortes. Day by day, Montezuma made more and more concessions, until he swore allegiance to the Spanish Emperor, Charles V. Soon he became a virtual prisoner of the Spaniards, and Cortes felt strong enough to attack the very basis of Aztec life: its religion. With a small group of men he went into one temple to overthrow the idols, some of

which were covered with congealed blood two or three inches thick. Feeling against the Spaniards became explosive.

At the same time Cortes had to march the two hundred and fifty miles to the coast to put down a threat to his authority by other Spaniards from Cuba. In less than a month, he was back. At once, the Mexican nobles deposed Montezuma, still a prisoner, and put his brother in his

place. Violent fighting broke out, in which Montezuma was killed. It continued until, in November 1521, Cortes found himself master of much of Central America.

He had accomplished this conquest in less than three years from the time he first landed in Mexico; partly through his own military gifts; partly through possessing superior weapons, cannons, steel swords and horses; and partly because other Indians were so resentful of being used as raw material for endless human sacrifices that they were prepared to help him against the Aztecs. Above all, he had succeeded because of the astonishing fact that Montezuma had not attempted to stop him.

Once Cortes had shown the way, an even more remarkable conquest followed. An illiterate soldier of fortune called Francisco Pizarro set sail from Panama in the first boats built by Western man for use on the Pacific. He had a hundred and eighty men and twenty-seven horses, and landed on the coast of Peru in 1532. From two earlier expeditions Pizarro had some idea of what he was up against: an empire ruled by people known as Incas, which stretched for three thousand miles, which had military roads and great fortresses and a highly organised system of absolute rule by one man. It sounded an impossible undertaking, but Pizarro, at nearly sixty years of age, decided to take what might be his last, desperate chance.

He needed to march through some of the most difficult country in the world, the high Andes, where men live and work at over twelve thousand feet and develop particular qualities of the lungs and the blood to enable them to adapt to the thin air. Ironically enough, he was only able to advance because of the wonderful Inca system of roads, and the rope bridges that were slung over deep mountain gorges, swaying alarmingly as anyone went across them. Where the mountains were too steep for roads, there were stairs for pack llamas to climb.

Once again the invading Spaniards found a civilisation at least as advanced in some respects as what they had left behind. The gold work was even finer and more prolific than in Mexico. The cities were well planned with wide, straight streets, and were built of huge blocks of slightly irregular stone, jointed together with extraordinary precision. There was more elaborate walling in the way that the steep mountains were terraced, and an elaborate system of irrigation enabled the most barren-looking mountain sides to bear crops.

The administration of this enormous empire was of military precision, but oddly enough the Incas lacked what we think of as a basic tool of civilisation. They had no system of writing, but they could keep detailed accounts and inventories by means of knots on a fringe of ropes, according to a method that nobody now understands.

Once again, it is astonishing that Pizarro and his handful of men could have defeated such a highly organised nation. The answer is, they were fortunate in the moment they chose. The ruler of the people was called simply 'the Inca' and the last great Inca had died in 1527. At the time when Pizarro landed, a power struggle had broken out between two of his sons, the legitimate successor, Huascar, and his more ruthless half-brother, Atahualpa. Huascar was defeated, but while Atahualpa was so engaged, Pizarro had already established his first colonial garrison.

Stories of the Spaniards' firearms and guns, of their animals larger than llamas, reached Atahualpa. He waited with fascination to meet Pizarro, serene in his confidence in his own absolute power. For the Inca was not merely the high priest of a god, he was godlike himself.

It may have been self-confidence in his divine position, or it may have been a more human wish not to show weakness, that led Atahualpa to meet Pizarro without arming any of his six thousand supporters. They met, with Atahualpa gorgeous in gold and turquoise, and then, at the moment when Pizarro dropped his handkerchief, the Spanish cannon boomed out, the arquebuses were fired, the sharp steel swords lunged at bare arms and legs. Atahualpa was captured, and the Spaniards sang joyfully, 'Rise, O Lord! and judge thine own cause'.

Atahualpa was told his life would be spared in return for gold and silver. At some time, the exact moment is not known, he managed to send secret instructions that Huascar should be murdered. He did not want the Spaniards to set up a rival Inca in his place. The gold came from temples that had doors covered with gold, bands of gold three feet high round the walls, and life-sized gold effigies. There was so much precious metal available that the Spaniards melted down a garden made of golden plants, and they used silver to shoe their horses. But it was not enough to save Atahualpa. He was tried on various charges, including worshipping idols, and executed.

The Spaniards advanced on Cuzco, the capital of the Incas, where the greatest treasures were to be found, and they looted it. To judge by the Inca work that survives, the artistic loss of what was melted down was immense. This was the gold that filled the many 'treasure ships' sent to Spain, which Drake and other Englishmen would attack later on in the century.

The lure of all this gold was so great that the new conquerors fell out among themselves, and Pizarro was assassinated ten years after his expedition began.

After the death of Atahualpa, the Spaniards had

crowned a young man called Manco as puppet Inca. Then he too revolted against them. He fled and took refuge in cities that the Spaniards never discovered. One of them was probably Machu Picchu, set among sheer, forested mountains, and overlooking gorges thousands of feet deep.

Machu Picchu is one of the most breath-taking sites in the world, with terraces, houses and temples clinging to the upper slopes of a sheer ridge. Nobody knew of its existence until, in 1911, it was discovered by an American called Hiram Bingham. Bingham thought that Machu Picchu must be the site of Vilcabamba, the legendary last refuge of the Incas, but some scholars disputed this.

Then in 1964 another American, Gene Savoy, discovered a lost Inca city that was overgrown with trees and vines and covered with tons of oozy, decayed vegetation. It is now thought that this may well be Vilcabamba.

Nobody knows for certain how many other Inca cities remain undiscovered. The Peruvians themselves have little money to excavate them.

The effects of Spanish rule fell heavily on the country. It took only a few generations to destroy the elaborate system of agriculture, to slaughter the great flocks of llamas, and to reduce the finely built cities to piles of filth in which the people died from new European diseases to which they had no resistance.

It is still astonishing that these conquests could ever have happened. Is the clue to be found in Montezuma's words when he talked of the strangers as coming back to their own kingdom? The reason for this lies at the heart of Aztec religion. They believed in a god called Quetzalcoatl, who came from the east and then disappeared to the east again. He was tall and white skinned, and had a flowing beard, a feature almost unknown among the native people of the Americas, who do not grow hair on their faces. He came, went, and it was believed he would come again. Was the arrival of the Spaniards, with their strange beasts and weapons, their ships with huge sails like birds' wings, the promised return of the gods?

One reason why Montezuma believed it might be was the Aztec calendar which divided the year into two hundred and sixty days. On the other hand, there was obviously also a solar year, which governed the crops, of three hundred and sixty-five days. The two systems came together every fifty-two years, so that the end of each cycle and the beginning of each new one was considered to be of grave importance.

It was at the start of a cycle that Cortes landed.

In the same way, the Incas had a legend of 'a white man, large of stature' who had disappeared over the waves. He was their creator god, called Viracocha, and when the Spaniards appeared some of the Indians called them 'Viracochas' because they too were white and came from the waves. Although there is no evidence that any of the Inca leaders identified the Spaniards with gods, the general atmosphere of superstitious foreboding can only have helped the Spaniards' cause.

The question which inevitably arises is whether Montezuma's belief had any basis at all in fact. Had there ever been a white visitor with a beard whose culture was so far in advance of the native Americans that he seemed godlike to them? At one point it was assumed that legends like this were no more than fairy tales. Then archaeologists began to wonder.

The story of the Flood is to be found in Babylonian legend as well as in the Bible, and certainly excavations show signs of very deep flooding in the land between the Tigris and the Euphrates.

The story of the lost continent of Atlantis attracted much wild speculation for many years, and then in 1967 a well preserved ancient city was found under volcanic ash in the Greek island of Thera. Since then it has been thought that a volcanic eruption, followed by a tidal wave which could have overwhelmed the great cities of Crete, may be the origin of this story of a lost continent.

If these legends, and others, have some foundation in fact, could there be any truth behind what Montezuma told the Spaniards?

The first question is whether white men had reached America long before Columbus. In the case of North America, there are strong grounds for thinking they did. The Norse sagas speak of settlements in a place called Vinland, which seems to be in America, and in 1960 a Norse settlement was found at a place called L'Anse aux Meadows in Newfoundland.

But Newfoundland is a long way from Mexico. If the Norsemen never went so far south, did even earlier white men do so? One suggestion is that the Phoenicians did. They were the greatest seamen of antiquity, and are known to have sailed through the Straits of Gibraltar to the Canary Islands, and there is argument as to whether or not they went so far out in the Atlantic as the Azores. Then it has been said that a tablet was found in Brazil, saying that men from the Phoenician city of Sidon had landed there, but no-one has seen the original.

In the absence of any proof, some historians have approached the question differently, and asked if the civilisations which Cortes and Pizarro found in America resembled any known civilisations in the Old World. The answer has been given that they resembled the Egyptian civilisation.

In all, no fewer than sixty points of similarity have been put forward. In both there was worship of a sun god, symbolised by a solar disc and by the use of three creatures in religious art: bird, snake, and cat. The kings claimed descent from the sun, and married their own sisters so as not to dilute the divine blood. The sun worshippers lived quite differently from other American Indians, who built huts of branches and leaves. Like the Egyptians, they built cities of stone and bricks, and showed immense skill in masonry.

The Olmecs, who preceded the Aztecs in Mexico, travelled long distances to find stone, instead of using timber that was easily available.

What is particularly striking is that these American people built pyramids. The pyramids now to be found in Mexico and Yutacan are arranged in huge steps like the Egyptian step pyramid at Saqqara, rather than the later and better-known pyramids of Giza which have straight sides. At one time it was thought that the American pyramids, unlike the Egyptian, served only as temples, but in 1952 the burial of a priest-king, complete with grave-goods, was found in a pyramid at Palenque in Mexico. The actual body was only a skeleton, but the art of mummifying, associated mainly with Egypt, was also practised in Peru.

One of the most remarkable features of American life before Columbus was the calendar used by the Mayans, the neighbours of the Aztecs, who lived on the Gulf of Mexico. They were able to measure time more accurately than their contemporaries in Europe, indeed more accurately than the calendar that we ourselves work by. Their astronomical year was calculated as having 365.2420 days, that is one day short in five thousand years, whereas our year of 365.2425 days gives one and a half days too much in the same length of time.

Their observations of Venus are judged to be equally accurate by modern astronomers. What is extraordinary is that this calendar goes back to 3113 B.C. The earliest Mayan document that is known only goes back to A.D. 320 and we have no idea what was happening in America at that date. 3113 B.C. is, however, the time when the first dynasty of Egypt was founded.

Other resemblances are the use of vegetable matter to make paper; many similarities in farming and fishing techniques; in weapons; in musical instruments; and in clothes.

Professor Marcel Homet has claimed there are close resemblances between the ancient Egyptian and the Mayan languages. Above all, there is the use of reed boats. The Egyptians made boats from papyrus, the reed from which paper is made. American Indians, even today, make boats from the reeds which grow around Lake Titicaca, twelve and a half thousand feet high on the borders of Peru and Bolivia.

Could these reed boats be not merely a resemblance but the actual link between the two civilisations? The immediate reaction is that this is quite impossible.

This is to underestimate the courage and ingenuity of one man, Thor Heyerdahl. He had already proved that Peruvians *could* have drifted across the Pacific on balsa rafts. Now he set out to prove that the Egyptians or other ancient peoples *could* have crossed the Atlantic.

He had a papyrus boat built, on the pattern shown in ancient Egyptian paintings, by men from Lake Chad in

Africa. They had built boats for inland waters, but never for ocean going, and so only added on the high stern, shown in the paintings, when Heyerdahl insisted.

In spite of many forebodings, the boat floated, and the reed did not become waterlogged. Heyerdahl and his companions, who included a black African and a Russian, managed to sail three thousand miles west across the South Atlantic before having to abandon their ship, *Ra*. When they did, it was largely because of weaknesses in the stern.

Heyerdahl did not give up. He had a second ship, *Ra II*, built, this time by men from Lake Titicaca. They sailed from the Atlantic coast of Morocco, near a city already ancient by the time of the Roman empire, with stonework that Heyerdahl thought resembled buildings in Mexico and Peru. Just under two months later, they landed in Barbados on the other side of the Atlantic.

It makes a splendid story of adventure, and proves that the Atlantic may have been less of a barrier, even to such a flimsy craft as a paper boat, than everyone had imagined. It does not, of course, prove that the Egyptians, or any other ancient people, did actually cross the Atlantic.

Those who oppose the theory point out the gap in dates. The earliest of the great stone buildings in Mexico, at Teotihuacan, probably date from the second century B.C., when the great days of Egyptian building were over, and most of the surviving work was done within the Christian era. In Peru, the first major city, Tiahuanaco, near Lake Titicaca, is sixth to tenth century A.D., while the Aztecs and Incas themselves were both recent peoples at the time of the Spanish conquest, having succeeded earlier civilisations.

One of the civilisations which preceded the Incas in

Peru were people known as the Nascas. Their land included arid plateaus up above the coast. They took the stones with which the land was littered, and for some reason they went to enormous trouble to lay them out in very long lines. One obvious answer is that the lines are roads, but that does not explain why there is a particular pattern, being laid out in parallel lines, some intersecting. Nor does it account for the outline shapes of creatures like birds being found there.

Another theory is therefore that the lines show the rising and setting points of certain stars, and the birds represent the planets. They would then have been used for astronomical observations, and would help a primitive people to keep tracks of the changing year and know when to plant their crops.

One very remarkable feature about these lines is that the full pattern of them can only be seen from the air, which means that the people who made them never really saw their own work. The extent and accuracy of the lines has now been fully revealed by aerial photographs, some of which make them appear like the runways of a giant airfield. The author Erich von Däniken has suggested that that is just what they are. The theory of Egyptian influence in America may sound a little startling, but compared to Däniken's ideas it is commonplace.

Däniken considered the civilisations of early America, and decided that they showed a degree of technical and mechanical skill completely beyond the capacities of primitive man. He looked, for example, at the masonry of the Inca walls. Some of the blocks are over a hundred tons heavy, and may have up to twelve corners, each of them not quite a right angle. This stone jigsaw for giants is fitted together with astonishing accuracy. Although it uses no mortar it still remains firm, and has withstood hundreds of years of earthquakes.

Other works which he considered are the stone heads made by the Olmecs, an early Mexican civilisation, which are up to eleven feet high and show men wearing what look like padded helmets. Even more remarkable are the statues on Easter Island, some over thirty feet high, which Däniken thought could never have been erected by the inhabitants of the island.

He then considered early American legend. The Incas, he said, told of a golden space craft that came from the stars. The Mexican story was of Quetzalcoatl, who came from the land of the rising sun. He looked at paintings in a Mayan temple at Palenque, and thought that one of them looked like an astronaut in a space craft. Then he put all these things together and decided that the ancient monuments of America had in fact been built by visitors from outer space whose spaceships had landed on these mountain airfields.

There are three entirely separate questions involved here. The first is, are there intelligent beings on other worlds? The likeliest argument in favour of there being is that of sheer mathematical probability. There are thought to be something like one hundred thousand million stars in our own galaxy, and there may be as many galaxies as there are stars. In the face of this it is obviously impossible to say categorically that other forms of living intelligence – whether higher than ours, lower than ours, or at any rate different – do not exist.

Dr Wernher von Braun, the architect of the American space programme, said that, 'On the basis of statistical and philosophical considerations, I am convinced of the existence of such advanced living beings. But I must emphasise that we have no firm scientific basis for this conviction.'

The second question is whether we can ever have any communication with these intelligent beings. Dr von Braun considered it very doubtful because of the enormous distances between our own and other solar systems, and the still greater distance between our galaxy and other galaxies. So far, our own explorations in space have not found any signs of life, but there are those who believe that other beings have been more successful in getting within range of us. This is the basis of a whole very considerable literature on UFOs or Unidentified Flying Objects.

Since the second World War there have been many stories of flying objects, sometimes called 'flying saucers', for which no obvious explanation can be found. 'Sometimes they have appeared upon radar screens, like the objects observed moving at over four thousand miles an hour by operators at the Naval Airfield in Maryland in January 1965. At other times they have been seen by eyewitnesses. In New Hampshire in the same year, fifty-eight people claimed to have seen a moving object, which glowed a bright, fiery red.

At around the same time, cases were reported from other parts of the world, such as Australia, Yugoslavia and Bulgaria.

Not surprisingly, this has led some people to talk of collective hysteria, a modern version of forms of religious hysteria found in earlier times. Another possibility is that it is some natural phenomenon. So far as our knowledge of space is concerned, we are very much at the beginning of an age of discovery. We are doing things, such as reaching the moon, which would have been thought impossible a few decades ago, and nobody can yet tell what lies ahead.

One example of how rapidly ideas are changing and developing in this field is the recent suggestion that there are 'black holes' in space. These are, in effect, collapsed stars, that exercise so great a force of gravity that they pull in all light and any matter around them, rather than giving light out. In Siberia, a great deal of damage was caused when something collided with the earth in 1908. It was assumed that this was a meteorite; more recently it was suggested that it was a flying saucer that then burnt up; the latest suggestion is that the earth came into collision with a black hole.

Finally, there is the question that *if* intelligent beings exist in the universe, *if* they have tried to get in touch with us, have we any grounds for believing that they helped to build the ancient monuments of America? What proof can Däniken offer to support his ideas?

It seems that his method of working is to soak himself in myths, sagas and the Bible, and thereafter to proceed by a sort of extra-sensory vision. He claims he 'steps out of time' and sees 'everything simultaneously – past, present and future'.

It is not surprising that this should have led to some violent criticism, particularly when his vision led him to describe a sacred library in a cave in Ecuador, a place where he had never actually been.

An article in the magazine *Encounter* for August 1973 describes him in terms like a 'paranoid dreamer'. It also admits that his 'fairy tales for adults' as it describes them have had world wide sales of over five and a half million copies, which may tell us less about Däniken than about ourselves.

The famous psychologist Jung said that belief in flying saucers shows a desire for help from outside the confines of a world that does not provide any answers at all for all the distress it causes us. Däniken himself admits this when he says, 'Another major reason for the success of my books is religious uncertainty.'

Apart from the Egyptians and spacemen, paper boats and flying saucers, what other explanations have been put forward for the achievements of ancient America? The traditional view is that both North and South America were originally populated by people from Asia. What is now the narrow Bering Strait between Siberia and Alaska was once dry land. According to this view, some of these people remained in a very primitive state, as do the inhabitants of the Amazon rain forests today, while others such as the Incas and Mayas achieved a high level of development without any outside help.

On the face of it, this seems a very dull theory: or is it? The existence of completely independent civilisations suggests an almost unlimited creativeness and ingenuity in the human race. It also shows that men everywhere are concerned with the problem of their origins and with trying to measure their place in the universe. To measure the stars and yet not make use of the wheel must seem to us nowadays an extraordinary sense of priorities, but it could have something to teach us about the nature of man.

A Room Without a Door

The castle was set high on the brow of a precipice. All around it towered mountains, covered with dense forest. The valley below was dark with impenetrable shadow. But mysterious as the castle looked from without, a more terrible mystery lay within its walls. What was hidden behind the curtain?

This is the setting of *The Mystery of Udolpho*, best known of the Gothic 'horror' novels. It was ridiculed by Jane Austen in *Northanger Abbey*, and imitated by countless writers since. Of course, such settings, such hidden secrets, bear very little relation to real life. Or do they occasionally? Is there a true horror story to be found in the ancient Scottish castle of Glamis, whose owners range back to Macbeth and down to the present day Earls of Strathmore, one of whom was the grandfather of Queen Elizabeth II?

On a television programme in 1962, Sir Brian Horrocks referred to the story that there was a secret room 'with a window but no doors', the entrance to which was known to only three people at any one time: the owner, his heir when he came of age, and the manager of the estate.

Other versions add the family lawyer to this list. Given the immensely thick walls of the castle, the idea of a secret room is quite plausible. Indeed, a party of young people once visited the castle and hung sheets and towels out of every window that they could find. There are over a hundred rooms, and they were sure they had visited every one, but, even so, when they had finished, no fewer than seven windows were left without any marking.

But this is not the end of the mystery. Sir Brian then said there is a *second* secret, somehow connected with the first. This second secret is also referred to in an article in *Notes and Queries* in 1908. The writer says that he heard it sixty years earlier, which means that it would have been current in the 1840's. How far back does it go?

It so happens that a young writer, deeply interested in Scottish history, visited Glamis in 1793. In a book called *Demonology and Witchcraft,* he describes the place. It was half empty, for 'the late Earl seldom resided there', and parts of it were furnished only with mediaeval suits of armour propped against cold, bare walls. The young man was told of a secret, 'a curious monument to the peril of feudal times, being a secret chamber, the entrance to which, by the law or custom of the family, must only be known to three persons at once'.

He was allowed to stay there for the night, and was put in a room off a winding stair, in an old four-poster bed with faded tartan hangings. 'I must own that when I heard door after door shut, after my conductor had retired, I began to consider myself as too far from the living, and somewhat too near the dead.' In the course of the night, he could meditate on the many violent happenings associated with Glamis. It is not surprising that he should feel 'that degree of superstitious awe which my countrymen call *eerie*'.

The young man's name was Walter Scott, and with the many historical novels that he was to publish, he did more to arouse an interest in Scottish history than any other person has ever done. These comments, made before he was famous, therefore have a particular interest.

It is noticeable that he refers to a secret; the room known to only three people, which might have been used as a hiding place at different times in Scotland's stormy past. He says nothing about a second secret at all. Did he not hear the legend? Or did only half the legend – the room – exist at that time, and did somebody later seek to take advantage of it? In other words, did something strange happen at Glamis between the 1790's, when Scott paid his visit, and the 1840's, when stories about a second secret were current? If so, it happened at a time when the family hardly lived there. Who were these absentee earls?

The man who had left Glamis deserted at the time of Scott's visit was John, the tenth earl. He did not marry until 1820, the day before he died. He married in hopes of legitimising his ten-year-old son, the child of a gardener's daughter, but under English law of that time the parents' subsequent marriage did not make the child legitimate. Ironically, had John been living at Glamis, Scottish law would have done so. Here is a minor scandal, but no real mystery.

John's younger brother, George, married, but died childless in 1806. So it was the third brother, Thomas, who in 1820 succeeded as the eleventh earl. He had been married twenty years earlier to a Hertfordshire girl called Mary Elizabeth Carpenter, whom he may have met while visiting relations in that county. She had a son, Thomas, who took the title of Lord Glamis when his father succeeded. His mother was dead by then.

Lord Glamis was married in 1820 to a girl called Charlotte Grimstead. According to Douglas's *Scots Peerage* and Cockayne's *Complete Peerage* they had a son who was born and died the same day the following year. Burke's *Peerage* gives the eldest son as being Thomas George, known as 'Ben', born in 1822. As births and deaths did not have to be registered until 1837, we cannot check the point. Another son, Claude, was born some two years later. Lord Glamis himself died while his father was still alive, so he never succeeded to the title. His children were brought up by their mother in England, and not at Glamis.

Ben became earl on the death of his grandfather in 1846. He married, but insisted on 'refraining from parenthood', and for this or some other reason he and his wife separated. She died at the age of twenty-eight; according to her nephew's wife of 'a broken heart', but according to her sister of peritonitis. Ben died childless in 1865, so his brother Claude became the thirteenth Earl of Strathmore. He was, by all accounts, a kind, conscientious man, who was married with five children. From the day of his succession, three very strange things happened.

The first was a startling change in the new Earl himself, thought to date from his having been told the secret of Glamis. Apparently, not being an eldest son, he had not heard it before. He said to his wife that they had often joked about it together, but now, 'I have been into the room, I have heard the secret, and if you wish to please me you will *never* mention the subject again.' A famous gossip, Augustus Hare, who visited the house, commented on how happy and lively the family were. 'Only Lord Strathmore himself has an ever sad look.'

The second happening was that a workman 'became alarmed' at something he saw along a passage near the chapel. The Earl was summoned from Edinburgh by tele-gram, and closely questioned the workman. 'He and his family were subsidised and induced to emigrate.' The third occurrence was a violent outbreak of haunting.

Glamis Castle has a long history of ghosts, as Scott had discovered. Their stories are interwoven with the violent history of the castle and Scotland itself. Nearly a thousand years ago, a Scottish king, Malcolm II, was murdered

there, and it is said that the floor has been boarded over to hide a blood stain that keeps on reappearing. The most famous 'thane of Glamis' is, of course, Macbeth, whom everyone associates with the supernatural.

Then there are stories about the ghost of the fifteenth-century Earl 'Beardie' who was playing cards with his heir when the Devil appeared. He swore a 'terrible oath' that he would play on till the game finished, if necessary to 'the

crack of doom'. Next comes Jonet Douglas, who was burnt at the stake as a witch and also for plotting against the life of King James V. She is said to reappear occasionally, with a red glow around her. There is a white lady, a grey lady, a lady without a tongue, as well as something that makes the sound of footsteps but has never been seen.

It is, perhaps, inevitable that stories like this should grow up in such a place, but now, in the 1860's, it was suddenly claimed that these phantoms had reappeared, almost as if they were trying to frighten the new owners away. The Bishop of Brechin heard of the haunting and offered to hold a service of exorcism. According to Augustus Hare, the Earl was deeply grateful, but said that 'in his unfortunate position no-one could help him'.

Whatever was it inside the room? What was the second secret that was preying on the Earl's mind? Here, we are right back in the world of the Gothic novel, which had reached new heights in *Jane Eyre* and its terrifying descriptions of some strange creature kept locked in an upper room, who proved to be Mr Rochester's mad wife. Did Glamis have a similar secret? If the writer in *Notes and Queries* had heard the rumours correctly, it did: not a mad wife, but the rightful heir. He was 'a monster . . . who is so unpresentable that it is necessary to keep him out of sight and out of possession'. It is not surprising that 'this terrible secret is said to have a depressing effect on the holder of the title (who, if the legend were exact, would not be in possession lawfully of either title or property) and on his heir.'

If this is so, who was it? From the ninth earl who died in 1776, to Claude who succeeded as thirteenth earl in 1865, everyone seems accounted for, with one exception: the child said to have been born and died the same day in 1821. This was the supposed first son of Lord Glamis and his wife, Charlotte Grimstead. Was there something strange about him?

Some inborn defects are not obvious at first sight, and the mother only realises gradually that her child is not making normal responses. It has been suggested that this fact lies behind the stories of changelings, children whom mothers claimed had been taken by the fairies and fairy children left in their place. It was an attempt to explain that the baby was different from what he had seemed at first.

But some other defects, such as gross deformities, are obvious from the moment of birth. Was the heir to Glamis Castle one of these unfortunate beings, and did his parents decide to hide him away? If so, was he cared for so devotedly that he lived on and on against all expectation? Was having seen him, and fear of producing another like him, the reason why his brother Ben would never have any children? Was it the sight of him that so changed his brother Claude? Was the trouble mental as well as physical, or, most bitter of all in a way, did Claude suspect that there might be a normal intelligence imprisoned in some grotesque form?

Claude's wife was due to have their sixth child in a few weeks. What terrors he must have felt, and how he must have relived his fears when each of their five remaining children was born. In his misery, he may even have brooded on a curse uttered by his ancestress, the ninth earl's widow, an odd woman who felt an 'unnatural hate' for her own eldest son, and wished her children 'unparalleled misery' if she was ever found to have deceived the Irish adventurer she married as second husband.

This is the solution to the mystery put forward by Paul Bloomfield in an article in *The Queen* magazine in 1964.

He also gives an interesting suggestion as to what may have been the cause of the trouble. He claims that Lord Glamis's mother, Mary Carpenter, was first cousin of Charlotte Grimstead, Lord Glamis's wife. Their common grandfather was John Walsh, variously described as a plumber and as a successful property speculator. In other words, the boy's parents were first cousins once removed.

Modern medical opinion is not against the marriage of cousins provided there is no hereditary defect on the side common to them both. If there is, obviously the chance of its being transmitted is doubled. As there is no other sign of defects being transmitted by the Bowes-Lyons, the family of the Earls of Strathmore, Paul Bloomfield thinks that the trouble may have come in the double dose of genes from the Walshes, a family about whom we know much less.

This theory about an unacknowledged heir may very well be the true explanation of the secret of Glamis. It leaves a number of other mysteries unanswered.

One is, what did the workman see that led Lord Strathmore to pay him to emigrate? Was it the 'monster' himself? If so, what form did his abnormalities take? They were probably something visible at first glance, and it has been suggested that he had no arms or legs, and his head was joined directly to his body. There is no proof of this at all.

The next question arises in 1876. The heir, who was later to be the father of Queen Elizabeth the Queen Mother, came of age and asked his father not to 'initiate' him into the family secret. Was it because he had seen the effect on his father, and did not feel he could bear the burden himself? Or was it a way of announcing to anybody round Glamis who may have suspected the truth that the secret no longer existed: in other words, that the heir had died, and the Earl of Strathmore was truly the earl in his own right at last?

Not everybody agrees with this. It has even been suggested that the hidden-away heir lived on to an immense age, and did not die until the early 1920's. Because of this refusal to hear the secret, nobody now knows how to enter the secret room, for all who once knew are dead.

A major question remains unanswered: the stories about the ghosts. These are recorded in *Lord Halifax's Ghost Book*, and were told to Lord Halifax by a highly respectable lady, Mrs Maclagan, the wife of the Archbishop of York. She was connected with the Bowes-Lyons since she had been the sister of Ben's wife, as well as having Lyons ancestry on her mother's side.

Mrs Maclagan declared it was common gossip that the Glamis ghosts had tried to scare Claude Bowes-Lyon and his family from making the place their home after he had inherited it in 1865. At one point, a whole house party is said to have been disrupted by them. One visitor woke up when she felt somebody bend over her and brush her face with his beard. A child woke, screaming that he had seen a giant. There was a crash of heavy furniture falling, and a dog howled.

Next night, the same crash was heard again at the same time, four o'clock. Other stories followed. Two visitors, the Dean of Brechin and the Provost of Perth, both claimed to have been visited by a tall figure who did not speak. A visitor called Mrs Wingfield saw a huge old man with a long, flowing beard, and although he breathed he had the face of a dead man.

Lady Strathmore, her nieces and another lady all saw a white lady flitting about in the avenue. At the time, they were all at different windows. The white lady herself was thought to be 'a most harmless apparition', but so many reports of haunting had a cumulative effect.

The agent for the estate, Andrew Ralston, who is thought to have been in the secret, refused to sleep a single night under the roof. One snowy night in 1869, he aroused gardeners and stablemen from their beds in order to dig out a path to his own house, a mile away. By 1887, Augustus Hare was reporting that Lord Strathmore had built a 'wing' to the castle. 'The servants will not sleep in the house, and the children are not allowed to do so.'

What lies behind the story of all these disturbances? One obvious possibility is that Ralston himself gave rise to them and encouraged them. If he was responsible for the invalid, for seeing that he was fed and given occasional fresh air, his problems must have increased enormously when the family went to live there. Instead of an empty, echoing castle, he had parties of guests and a large group of lively children. How much easier to scare them away.

The other possibility is to admit that there *was* some form of psychic disturbance inside the castle. If so, what was the nature of it? One answer is to accept the stories about the ghosts. Many people believe that the dead can reappear in a visible form, and cite famous cases of hauntings as evidence of this. One instance is the two ladies from Oxford who claimed to have seen people from the time of Louis XVI in the grounds of Versailles. Another is the nun whom many people claim to have seen around Borley Rectory. This house, now burnt down, has also been associated with strange sounds and smells, writing appearing on the wall, objects like bottles flying about, and unexplained outbreaks of fire.

Other people will disagree strongly, and say that such things are not possible: in fact almost any group of people is good for an argument about ghosts. What often emerges from such a discussion is that many who do not believe in actual ghosts think that the atmosphere of a place can be influenced by happenings in the past. Some, but by no means all, churches have a positive atmosphere of holiness, so do some ancient sacred places like Delphi.

Other places may seem impregnated with feelings of misery or of evil. There are people who claim to have felt this in old prisons, and also in places out in the open country and ordinary-looking suburban houses. Is it possible that Glamis Castle was affected by all that had happened there in the past? If so, was something that was latent within the castle suddenly aroused, so that everyone who went there was aware of a deep mental uneasiness, that took the form of claiming to see ghosts? If this is so, what triggered it off? Was it the worries and guilt of the Earl who now knew himself to be an innocent usurper, but who could not betray the truth without condemning his own family? Was it the misery of the creature who should have been in his place?

There are two completely separate questions here. Did something strange really happen at Glamis Castle? More important, do we believe that there are powers completely beyond our powers to see and grasp? This is the greatest mystery of them all.

The Fortune Teller

One of the greatest mysteries is whether or not we can have any knowledge of the future. Here, to end with, is a short story about a fortune teller.

One day about two hundred years ago, two young cousins in the island of Martinique went to have their fortunes told by an old Negress called Euphemia David. They went at dusk, walking through the sugar cane, and along a path bordered by giant lilies, to the shack where the old woman lived. The little girls were Creoles, that is Europeans born in the West Indies, and both had very high-sounding French names: Marie-Joseph Rose de la Pagerie, and Aimée Dubucq de Rivery.

Both girls were told what sounded like incredible stories. Marie-Joseph would marry; have two children; be widowed; live through a revolution; and then marry again. Now came the surprising part. Her second husband would be a dark, insignificant-looking man, who nevertheless would fill the world with his glory, and be bowed down to as a great conqueror. Marie-Joseph herself would become a queen, but in the end would be cast aside and would die unhappy.

Aimée's fate would be even more strange. She would be sent to Europe to finish her education, but her ship would be seized by corsairs, and she would be captured and imprisoned in a seraglio. There she would give birth to a son, who would reign gloriously, while she herself would never know outward honours, but would rule supreme in a great palace. Then, at the hour of her triumph, she would die a lingering death.

The one girl, Marie-Joseph, set off for Europe, where she was to be married to a French nobleman called the Vicomte de Beauharnais. At the moment she left Martinique, the first part of the old woman's prophecy came true. She had said that a light would appear in the heavens when the girl sailed, and the electrical discharge, known as St Elmo's fire, did appear round the masts of her ship. Marie-Joseph was duly married, and was thereafter known as Joséphine de Beauharnais. She had two children and survived the terror of the French Revolution, but was widowed when her husband was guillotined.

Two years later she made a rather surprising marriage to a little Corsican who apparently had nothing to commend him except for his rapid rise through the ranks of the French Army. His name was Napoleon Bonaparte.

The main source for this story is a book by a professional fortune teller in France, Anne-Marie Lenormand, with whom Joséphine was intimate. It is suspect because the book was not published until after Joséphine's death, when it would have been easy enough to alter the story to fit the events.

However, many people claimed to have heard her speak of the prophecies before they came true. Sir Walter Scott said she was telling the story very soon after her marriage, at which point nobody could have foreseen that Napoleon would become Emperor of France, and one of the great conquerors of history. She was also, while she was a powerful Empress, speaking of the unhappy end that Euphemia David had predicted. True enough, Napoleon divorced her, because they had no children.

What became of the other girl? Her life was much less public, much less documented than Joséphine's, so nobody had the same interest in trying to prove that the prophecy came true.

As foretold, she was sent to school in France, and when she sailed homewards to the West Indies, her ship foundered. The passengers were rescued by a Spanish boat, and taken towards Majorca, but within sight of the island they were captured by Algerian pirates.

Aimée, who was beautiful in a pink and white way that was a rarity to the Arabs, was recognised as a magnificent prize. So great was her value that she was presented to the Sultan of Turkey for his harem. The rest of her life was spent shut up in a splendid prison, the Seraglio at Constantinople. She attracted the favour of the Sultan and bore a son, who later became the Sultan Mahmoud II. Aimée herself had the title of the Sultan Valideh, the Sultan's mother.

In the strange, secret world of the Seraglio, the sultan Valideh could wield a great deal of influence, for the Sultan himself had no queen. All that we know about Aimée suggests that she managed to keep her own identity and her own loyalty in these exotic surroundings, and when she died the Sultan had a Catholic priest fetched to her bedside. How great was the extent of her influence, especially at one very vital moment, is another mystery in itself.

During Mahmoud's reign, the Turks started to turn a

little towards the West, and to alter some aspects of their traditional way of life. They did not, however, look to friendship with France, but with England. In particular, they signed a peace treaty with Russia in the very moment of the Napoleonic wars that freed part of the Russian Army to fight Napoleon, who was then advancing towards Moscow. His retreat from Moscow proved to be a turning point in his life. And in history.

It may well have been the influence of the British Minister, Stratford Canning, that led to this treaty, but another reason has been suggested. Did the Sultan Valideh remember that once she was a little French girl in Martinique, who had visited an old fortune teller with her cousin; and did she now seek to avenge herself for that same cousin whom Napoleon had discarded as Empress of France? Who knows?

Acknowledgements and Suggestions for Further Reading

I would like to acknowledge the kind help of Dr Howard Somervell and Mr Showell Styles for providing information, and Mr Richard Hough and Mrs Elizabeth Attenborough for suggesting useful sources.

I have read many books and articles in magazines in the course of research for the writing of this book. The following is a list of the books and magazines from which I have drawn material. In some cases I have also quoted briefly from them.

Death by Witchcraft
Fabian, Robert, *Fabian of the Yard* (Heirloom Modern World Library, 1955)
McCormick, Donald, *Murder by Witchcraft* (John Long, 1968)

In Search of the Lost World
Fawcett, Lt Col P. H., Fawcett, Brian (ed.), *Exploration Fawcett* (Hutchinson, 1953)
Fleming, Peter, *Brazilian Adventure* (Jonathan Cape, 1933, Penguin, 1957)
Furneaux, Robin, *The Amazon* (Hamish Hamilton, 1969)

Is it Abominable?
Bonington, Chris, *Annapurna South Face* (Cassell & Co, 1971)
Hillary, Sir Edmund, *High Adventure* (Hodder & Stoughton, 1955)

Smythe, Frank S., *The Valley of Flowers* (Hodder & Stoughton, 1938)

Ward, Michael, *In This Short Span* (Victor Gollancz, 1972)

The Guardian of the Treasure

de Sède, Gérard, *Le Trésor Maudit de Rennes-le-Château* (J'ai Lu, 1967)

By the Pricking of my Thumbs

Besterman, Theodore, *Water Divining* (Methuen, 1938)

de France, Le Vicomte Henry, *The Elements of Dowsing,* translated by A. H. Bell (Bell, 1948)

Underwood, Guy, *The Pattern of the Past* (Museum Press, 1969)

Who Stole the Necklace?

Mossiker, Frances, *The Queen's Necklace* (Victor Gollancz, 1961)

Can We Believe our Eyes?

Lee, Arthur Gould, *No Parachute* (Hutchinson, 1968)

McKee, Alexander, *The Friendless Sky* (Souvenir Press, 1962)

Robertson, Bruce (editor), *Air Aces of the 1914–1918 War* (Harleyford, 1970)

Banquets for the Dead

Bloch, Raymond, *The Ancient Civilisation of the Etruscans,* translated by James Hogarth (Barrie and Rockcliff, 1969)

Herodotus, *The Histories,* translated by Aubrey de Sélincourt (Penguin, 1954)

Lawrence, D. H., *Etruscan Places* (Martin Secker, 1932)

Pallottino, Massimo, *The Etruscans,* translated by J. Cremona (Penguin, 1955)

Strong, Donald, *The Early Etruscans* (Evans, 1968)

Wellard, James, *The Search for the Etruscans* (Cardinal, 1973)

A Malady in the Blood

Massie, Robert K., *Nicholas and Alexandra* (Victor Gollancz, 1968)

Paper Boats and Flying Saucers

Hemming, John, *The Conquest of the Incas* (Macmillan, 1970)

Heyerdahl, Thor, *The Ra Expeditions* (George Allen & Unwin, 1971)

Innes, Hammond, *The Conquistadors* (Collins, 1969)
von Däniken, Erich, *Chariots of the Gods* (Souvenir Press, 1969)

A Room Without a Door
Bloomfield, Paul, *Laying the Ghost of Glamis* (*The Queen*, December 1964)
Lindley, Charles, Viscount Halifax, *Lord Halifax's Ghost Book* (Geoffrey Bles, 1936)
Underwood, Peter, *A Gazetteer of British Ghosts* (Souvenir Press, 1971)

The Fortune Teller
Blanch, Lesley, *The Wilder Shores of Love* (John Murray, 1954)

As well as these books on particular subjects, many of the mysteries are referred to in newspapers of the appropriate date. In particular, back copies of *The Times* and an index to the newspaper can be found in many reference libraries.

More Beaver Books

We hope you have enjoyed this Beaver Book. Here are some of the other titles:

A Knight and his Castle   What was it like to live in a castle, by R. Ewart Oakeshott

The Twelve Labours of Hercules   The adventures of the hero Hercules, beautifully retold by Robert Newman; illustrated superbly by Charles Keeping

Travel Quiz   A brain-teasing quiz book for all the family on all aspects of travel by plane, train and car

My Favourite Animal Stories   Sad, funny and exciting stories about all sorts of animals, chosen and introduced by Gerald Durrell

The Call of the Wild   The epic story of Buck the great sledge dog in the frozen North, by Jack London

The Last of the Vikings   Henry Treece's exciting story, in the saga tradition, about the young Harald Hardrada, King of Norway; with more superb illustrations by Charles Keeping

Ghost Horse   Dramatic story about a legendary stallion in the American West, by Joseph E. Chipperfield

New Beavers are published every month and if you would like the *Beaver Bulletin* – which gives all the details – please send a stamped addressed envelope to:

Beaver Bulletin
The Hamlyn Group
Astronaut House
Feltham
Middlesex TW14 9AR

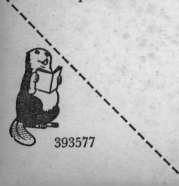

393577